Y0-BDA-606

EFFECTIVE SCHOOLING FOR ECONOMICALLY DISADVANTAGED STUDENTS: SCHOOL-BASED STRATEGIES FOR DIVERSE STUDENT POPULATIONS

Social and Policy Issues in Education: The University of Cincinnati Series

Kathryn M. Borman, Series Editor

Contemporary Issues in U.S. Education, *edited by Kathryn M. Borman, Piyush Swami, and Lonnie D. Wagstaff*

Early Childhood Education: Policy Issue for the 1990s, edited by Dolores Stegelin

Effective Schooling for Disadvantaged Students: School-based Strategies for Diverse Student Populations, *edited by Howard Johnston and Kathryn M. Borman*

Home Schooling: Political, Historical, and Pedagogical Perspectives, *edited by Jane Van Galen and Mary Anne Pitman*

in preparation

Assessment Testing and Evaluation in Teacher Education, *edited by Suzanne W. Soled*

Basil Bernstein: Consensus and Controversy, *edited by Alan R. Sadornik*

Children Who Challenge the system, *edited by Anne M. Bauer and Ellen M. Lynch*

Explaining the School Performance of Minority Students: Anthropological Perspectives, *edited by Evelyn Jacob and Cathie Jordan*

EFFECTIVE SCHOOLING FOR ECONOMICALLY DISADVANTAGED STUDENTS: SCHOOL-BASED STRATEGIES FOR DIVERSE STUDENT POPULATIONS

J. Howard Johnston
University of South Florida

Kathryn M. Borman
University of Cincinnati

ABLEX PUBLISHING CORPORATION
NORWOOD, NEW JERSEY

LC
4069.3
.J64
1992

Library of Congress Cataloging-in-Publication Data

Johnston, J. Howard
    Effective schooling for economically disadvantaged students :
school-based strategies for diverse student populations / J. Howard
Johnston, Kathryn M. Borman.
       p.   cm.—(Social and policy issues in education)
    Includes bibliographical references and index.
    ISBN 0-89391-720-6
    1. Socially handicapped children—Education. I. Borman, Kathryn
M. II. Title. III. Series.
LC4069.3.J64 1990
371.96'7—dc20   91-46595
                                                CIP

Ablex Publishing Corporation
355 Chestnut Street
Norwood, New Jersey 07648

This book is dedicated to the Urban Appalachian Council and to the United Way/Community Chest which supports it and other excellent local, community-based programs everywhere.

Table of Contents

Preface

Disadvantage is an elusive term. Lawmakers and policymakers have wrestled with legal definitions that are suitable for defining government- or foundation-sponsored social programs; educators struggle with the concept as it applies to student preparation for conventional learning; and social scientists are concerned about its qualities as an operational definition for identifying populations for study. All of these groups focus their attention on disadvantage for the same reasons: to ameliorate its effects on people, particularly children. Regardless of the orientation each group brings to the term, then, it is the *effect* of economic disadvantage which must capture the attention of the groups with vested interest in the welfare of our collective citizenry. Thus, for our purposes, economic disadvantage is the sustained existence of poverty in such a degree as to preoccupy a family and to affect its ability to improve its condition.

During the 1980s, the emblems of economic disadvantage have loomed larger. The gulf between poverty and affluence has deepened and widened; the images of poverty—the homeless, the hungry, the displaced elderly, the sick—are brought to our home television screens with powerful and alarming regularity; the promise of a secure economic future is denied to an increasing number of youth in America. At the same time, tantalizing images of material wealth are held out to our children, many of whom, regardless of their current economic status, will not fare as well as their parents. The result is that fewer and fewer of America's youth believe that conventionally legitimate means to success, such as schooling, are still viable methods for securing their futures.

Poor and minority youth, in particular, find that schooling may not pay off in the long run. The history of unemployment and poverty found in poor communities demonstrates conclusively to many children that the effects of schooling, no matter how highly they may be touted, are insufficient to overcome the overwhelming odds against their full participation in American economic life. Furthermore,

schools in communities of poor and minority families have, historically, been less effective in producing desirable educational outcomes.
Thus, the evidence for commitment to schooling is weak and the
evidence against it is compelling.

Although the problems of educating disadvantaged youth often
seem overwhelming, this volume speaks with a certain amount of
optimism on the subject. All the authors are committed to the
principle that disadvantaged children *can* be served by schools.
Granted, the writers recommend major policy changes, dramatic
alterations of school structures and practices, and fundamentally
different ways of viewing both disadvantaged youth and effective
schooling, but each author expresses a fundamental faith that America can educate its children...all of them.

This volume models one of the major themes of its contributors: an
interdisciplinary approach to research and a collaborative approach to
school-based interventions. The contributors include sociologists, psychologists, anthropologists, linguists, policy analysts, and educators.
The topics include family involvement in schooling, linguistic contexts of schooling, political and social policy analyses, school practices,
and the role of foundations in supporting school improvement. The
focal groups include young children, young and older adolescents,
ethnic and linguistic minorities, and families.

When the collective attention of researchers from different disciplines, school personnel, and policymakers is focused on an educational problem, it begins a dislogue that promises improvement. This
volume's collection of chapters is designed to be among the first to
provide the substance for a productive dialogue.

The volume is organized into three sections. Part I, Policy and
Disadvantaged Youth, includes three chapters. The first, "Identifying
the Problem of Educational Disadvantage" by John Ralph, wrestles
with a major issue facing both policymakers and educators, namely,
the multiple problems associated with a deceptively simple question:
"Do we know whom to help?" Sources of confusion surrounding this
question include the conflicting array of statistical indicators of
disadvantagement and the multiple problems associated with disadvantaged youth such as growing up in an economically depressed
inner-city neighborhood, escalating rates of pregnancy, and financially
strapped central-city schools. Ralph concludes that, although there are
promising trends such as increased academic gains among disadvantaged school populations, all indications are that schools will require
even more resources in the future to keep pace with the increasing
numbers of students needing support for sustained educational
progress.

A current target for federal support is early childhood education for disadvantaged young children and their families. In her chapter, "Implementing Programs and Policies for Young Children and their Families," Sharon L. Kagan traces the historical development of the federal government's early childhood education policies. Policy development, she concludes, has been hampered by a number of factors including the longstanding division between policies regarding child care and policies addressing educational needs of children. Most programs are fragmented, lack coherence, and are constantly plagued by a host of critics who argue that the United States is too vast and diverse a society to allow any comprehensive policy to be effective. Kagan argues that in the decade of the 1990s, policy will likely be guided by a vision of program implementation at the local level. However, she also asserts that the federal government must take responsibility for chronicling and diffusing information on innovative practices, fulfilling its important role in providing leadership and resources.

The last of the three chapters included in Part I of the volume addresses the important question: "Private Foundations: What Is Their Role in Improving the Education of Disadvantaged Youth?" M. Hayes Mizell, director of the Program on Disadvantaged Youth of the Edna McConnel Clark Foundation, and author of the chapter sadly notes that foundations have generally been reluctant to direct resources to public schools and school systems, often fearing that activities supported by these dollars would be undermined by the system's array of bureaucratic, political, and financial problems. Although educational reform through school restructuring may provide a strategy to insure the success of programs for disadvantaged students, it is not as yet clear to many foundations' board members that this strategy will work as reformers believe it will. While some philanthropists are waiting in the wings, others such as those affiliated with Mizell's organization are recognizing the importance in supporting school-based restructuring reforms aimed ultimately at assisting disadvantaged students.

The second section of the volume, Families and Communities, focuses on linkages among children's learning in schools, families, and community-based agencies and programs. In the first chapter in this section, "Critical Factors in Why Disadvantaged Students Succeed or Fail in School," Reginald M. Clark analyzes a question as important as those raised by the authors of the volume's earlier chapters. Not all children who are identified as disadvantaged fail to achieve in school. It is crucial to understand why some succeed and others fail. Using data from his close observational studies of high achieving ten-year-olds and adolescents, Clark identifies activities associated with success in school. Clark's ongoing research is allowing us to understand the important connections between time spent learning in school and in the home and community.

The second chapter in this section is "Mediating School Cultural Knowledge For Children: The Parents' Role," by Concha Delgado-Gaitan and Martha Alexsaht-Snider. The authors use the Vygotskian notion of "proximal development" to explain the importance to the academic success of their children of Mexican-American parents' role as mediators of learning. Delgado-Gaitan and Allexsaht-Snider's study of children's interactions with parents in the context of carrying out homework assignments demonstrates that the parent is the most knowledgeable adult about the child's current capacities as well as the potential for cognitive development. When children are helped through their school-related problems by a parent who also understands the school's demands, children become more functional in the classroom. The strategies outlined in the chapter require extremely high levels of home-school communication and cooperation with both parents and teachers deeply involved in carrying out a program for children's academic learning.

It is clear from both chapters included in this section that uniformity in policy addressing disadvantaged students is likely to exacebate conditions which lead to educational disadvantage and ultimate school withdrawal. Indeed, the diversity that exists in disadvantaged populations and the ways these differences relate to formal education calls for policy which permits the creation of local remedies and options.

In the final section of this volume, Schools and Schooling examines existing school practices that affect the performance of disadvantaged and minority students in existing school structures. Focusing initially on the simple fact of moving from one school to another, Howard Johnston examines the adjustment difficulties faced by students moving from elementary to middle schools. Using Hirschi's social bonding theory as a springboard, Johnston identifies the incongruities between the family norms of disadvantaged children and the norms established in highly authoritative school structures. Further, he traces sources of anxiety experienced by children about to make the transition from the primary or elementary school. Unlike the earlier transition, a successful move to middle school is predicated upon children's status, success, and achievement all of which are almost exclusively dependent upon academic performance. By studying the concerns of both high- and low-achieving youngsters about to enter middle-level schools, and comparing them with the concerns of disadvantaged youth slated to attend an alternative school, Johnston concludes that the social organization of the school is a primary determinant of the extent to which disadvantaged youth adjust to the social organization of education at the middle school level.

Continuing this theme, Roger Collins explores the difference between high- and low-resolution classrooms, and the ways in which teachers in each setting conceive of students' ability to learn. High-resolution classrooms, in which the teacher dominates instructional and social decisions, tend to exhibit characteristics associated with the belief that ability is a fixed, barely alterable phenomenon. The public nature of academic performance in this setting also tends to invite social comparisons. In low-resolution classrooms, where students are somewhat more autonomous and student choice is a major determinant of instructional activity, teachers tend to believe that ability is much more complex, differentiated, and incremental, and social comparisons are not invited. Collins observes that teacher education programs that emphasize the technology of teaching and the management of group learning prepare teachers for high-resolution classrooms and discourage them from working comfortably in low-resolution classrooms.

Finally, in her chapter, "Friendly or Unfriendly Text: A Comparison of Oral Dialogue of Economically Disadvantaged Children and the Written Dialogue of Early Literacy Materials," Johanna DeStefano gives close attention to how language use, sociocultural group, literacy materials, and literacy learning events in home and at school interact to contribute to higher rates of failure to achieve literacy. In her research of Tom, Dick, and Harry's experiences with "school dialogue" and home talk and children's literature, DeStefano identifies several gaps and inconsistences. This study is important because it demonstrates how schools and basal readers ignore the resources children bring from home to school in the primary grades. DeStefano's work is of critical importance in defining the variables, such as basal texts, over which educators have control and can change to build, in DeStefano's words, "bridges to literacy."

Taken as a set, the chapters in this volume lead the reader through issues, complexities, and strategies associated with local and school-based attempts to alleviate the effects of economic disadvantage on educational performance. All of the authors call for attention to a complex mix of social issues, policy issues, and school practices in order to achieve educational equity. All of them, though, are optimistic that this nation can achieve a system that educates all of its children. After all, they deserve nothing less.

J. Howard Johnston
Kathryn M. Borman
Cincinnati, Ohio
1990

Acknowledgments

The editors wish to express their appreciation to Piyush Swami and Lonnie R. Wagstaff for their support of the College of Education Symposium Series at the University of Cincinnati that resulted in the chapters included in this volume. In addition, the help and assistance of Patric Leedom is gratefully acknowledged. Ivan Charner of the Academy for Educational Development kindly assisted in making Reginald M. Clark's chapter available. We also acknowledge the cheerful assistance of Dale Wilburn in preparing this volume and the help of Barbara Bernstein of Ablex who is always supportive of our efforts.

Contributors

Martha Allexsaht-Snider: Martha Allexsaht-Snider works in the area of bilingual education at the University of Georgia. Her current research focuses on the interactive context of teacher-parent communication in schools serving minority populations.

Reginald M. Clark: Reginald Clark is a consultant to school systems working on improving home-school relations. He has also been a consultant to the U.S. Department of Education and the Education Commission of the States. Dr. Clark is author of *Family Life and School Achievement: Why Poor Black Children Succeed or Fail*, University of Chicago Press.

Roger L. Collins: Roger Collins is on the Educational Foundations faculty at the University of Cincinnati. His published works address the impact of school desegregation policies on poor and minority students and the impact of teacher-created learning environments on minority students.

Concha Delgado-Gaitan: Concha Delgado-Gaitan is a member of the graduate education faculty at the University of California, Davis. Her research has focused on the relationship between home and school and the involvement of parents in their children's education. Her most recent book is *Literacy for Empowerment: The Role of Parents in Children's Education*, published by The Falmer Press.

Johanna S. DeStefano: Johanna DeStefano is professor of language, reading, and literacy education at the Ohio State University. Her research focuses upon the social issues connected with literacy failure upon the social issues connected with literacy failure rates among disadvantaged youth. Her recent book, *Language, The Learner and The School*, addresses that set of issues.

J. Howard Johnston: Howard Johnston is professor of Secondary Education at the University of South Florida. His primary research interest is on the performance of disadvantaged youth in middle level schools. His most recent book is *The New American Family and the School*, published by the National Middle School Association.

Sharon L. Kagan: Sharon Kagan is associate director of the Bush Center in Child Development and Social Policy at Yale University. She has authored and edited numerous works on childhood education and policy; among them is *Children, Families and Government: Perspectives on American Social Policy.*

M. Hayes Mizell: Hayes Mizell is director of the Program on Disadvantaged Youth of the Edna McConnel Clark Foundation. He was appointed by President Carter to chair the National Advisory Council on the Education of Disadvantaged Children and currently serves on the board of the National Committee for Citizens in Education.

John Ralph: John Ralph is an education statistician at the National Center for Educational Statistics where he is involved in analysis and planning for the Department of Education's initiatives on effective schooling for disadvantaged youth.

Part I
Policy and Disadvantaged Youth

Identifying the Problem and Trends of Educationally Disadvantaged Students*

John Ralph

DO WE KNOW WHOM TO HELP?

David Ellwood, an economist who studies labor force issues and welfare reform, has argued that effective welfare policies must distinguish among the different needs of low-income families. By generalizing across diverse types of family poverty—for example, poor two-parent families in which the father works, poor female-headed families in which the mother may work part-time, and homeless families in which no one works—policymakers obscure the needs of the persons they mean to help. Ellwood's point is that there are no generic poor, and therefore no single, unified welfare policy will work for all poor families (Ellwood, 1988).

This argument holds a valuable lesson for educators too. When the clientele of social programs qualify for participation based on a single criterion such as family's socioeconomic level or, more common for educators, low school achievement, their needs will vary. Disadvantaged youth aren't all the same. Some youth need alternative or innovative approaches to education while others, perhaps even the majority, simply need added help. Effective policymaking identifies

---

* This chapter is intended to promote the exchange of ideas among researchers and policymakers. The views are those of the author, and no official support by the U.S. Department of Education is intended or should be inferred.

differences among program clientele, assesses their actual needs, and then provides access to appropriate program services and resources.

Economic policymakers have at least one advantage over educators: they know how to define a low-income family. In the 1960s economists agreed to the Orshansky index (Orshansky, 1965) as a measure of the threshold level of income for a family in poverty, a formula which holds still today. By contrast, educators have reached no consensus about who constitutes the population of disadvantaged students.[1] Since disadvantaged students have been the traditional clients of federal aid programs, it is surprising that no clear conception of educational disadvantagement has emerged to guide these programs, much less provide criteria to identify individual needs.

Take, for example, Chapter 1 LEA—the major federal program for economically and educationally disadvantaged students. Chapter 1's 1990 budget was $4.5 billion, and it served approximately 5 million students. Classroom observation studies find that, on average, students gain only about 10 minutes of instruction in reading or math on a day when they receive Chapter 1 services (Rowan & Guthrie, 1989). In the view of Launor Carter, the principal investigator of the Sustaining Effects Study of Title I (Chapter 1's predecessor), "[Title I] did not represent a unified or coherent treatment program...Title I was better defined as a funding program than as an educational treatment" (1984).

The distribution formula for Chapter 1 dollars reveals a fuzzy notion of whom the educationally disadvantaged are. Virtually every school district in the nation and over 90% of all schools receive some federal funds for disadvantaged students, including schools which by national standards are relatively wealthy (Birman, Orland, Jung, Anson, & Garcia, 1987). Within each district, individual schools receive funds based on the number of poor families they serve, and individual students are eligible on the basis of poor educational performance—determined usually by low achievement test scores. This crazy-quilt approach leads to neither poor families nor low-performing students being adequately served. Evaluation studies have found some schools providing Chapter 1 services though they have few low-income students and few low-achieving students, while other schools with high poverty concentrations and many low-achieving students are not providing program services (Ascher, 1987). The Sustaining Effects

---

[1] Bereiter (1985) has written that "after two decades of acrimonious debate, practically everyone today avoids the issue of educational disadvantagement...[We should] simply accept the fact that youngsters vary greatly in how much help they need and why. From this point of view, a successful compensatory education program is one that gives students plenty of help in learning." Another point of view is found in Ralph (1989).

Study estimated that "The absolute number of children receiving CE [compensatory education] who are non-poor and achieving higher than one year below grade level is greater than the number of children receiving CE services who fall below these cutoffs" (Carter, 1983, p. I-2).

WHY IS THE TERM "DISADVANTAGED YOUTH" SO POORLY DEFINED?

Attempts to specify meaningfully the population of disadvantaged youth bumps against three kinds of problems. The first is that many educators disagree about what disadvantagement *should* mean. Should disadvantaged youth include children predicted to fall behind based on socioeconomic factors? And, if so, how are principals to collect the kind of family and socioeconomic data necessary to calculate a reliable measure of students' backgrounds? Should disadvantaged children comprise only those who have already fallen behind in their school work?[2] After resolving what disadvantagement should mean, principals are often reluctant to enforce a criterion which limits their discretionary authority to place children in programs requested by parents or teachers. For these reasons, participation in compensatory education programs has been based on loose criteria of eligibility. Local program evaluators frequently find that differences in students' backgrounds explain why some "compensatory education" programs produce better results than others (Ralph & Dwyer, 1988).

The second difficulty to specifying terms like disadvantaged or at-risk youth lies in the tactical advantage of making them as broadly inclusive as possible. Program advocates writing reform-minded reports often want more program funds for youth from low-income families, youth from inner-city or minority families, migrant youth, bilingual youth, youth from single-parent families, youth who are single parents, handicapped youth, youth who have attempted suicide, youth who use drugs, and high school dropouts. By including such diverse groups, compensatory education broadens its public and political support—a strategy which has been remarkably successful (Ralph, 1989). Chapter 1's popularity among Congressmen and educators is

---

[2] An example of building from an explicit definition is found in the work of Pallas, Natriello, and McDill (1989, pp. 16-17). Educationally disadvantage means having been exposed to inappropriate educational experiences as indicated by poor achievement in school and correlated with "minority racial/ethnic group identity, living in a poverty household, living in a single-parent family, having a poorly educated mother, and having a non-English language background."

stronger today than when it first began, yet major evaluation studies of Title I and Chapter 1 have consistently shown that compensatory education has little or no enduring impact on learning once youngsters leave the program.[3]

A third source of confusion over who's disadvantaged stems from the variety of statistical indicators that analysts cite. To demonstrate the worsening problems of disadvantaged youth, researchers sometimes cite the growth of federal programs, such as the expanded number of students who qualify for Migrant Aid or Bilingual Aid. Another type of indicator relies on patterns of demographic growth to show that certain population subgroups, such as blacks or Hispanics or children from single-parent households, are growing more rapidly than majority population groups. For example, Harold Hodgkinson's 1985 monograph, *All One System,* used this approach when he urged educators to prepare for the year 2000 when "one of every three of us will be nonwhite." A third type of indicator simply reports on trends in the prevalence of "at risk" behavior among all youth. Increases in the number of school dropouts or births to unmarried teenagers in themselves are meant to reflect growing disadvantagement for youth.

In sum, without clear definitions, consistent program criteria, or specific data, the problems of disadvantaged youth are sometimes equated with the expanding problems plaguing all youth. Nationally representative data sets seldom have sample sizes sufficient to analyze at-risk trends for subgroups—such as low-income or minority or urban youth—but the available data can test whether youth on the whole are exhibiting greater or lesser amounts of at-risk behavior. On the assumption that rising levels of at-risk behavior will mean worsening problems for disadvantaged youth, the next section reviews the national data for school-related at-risk behavior. Where possible, trends for historically disadvantaged subgroups—youth from low-income families or minority families or youth from urban neighborhoods—will be reported separately.

ARE EDUCATIONALLY DISADVANTAGED YOUTH WORSE OFF TODAY?

According to newspaper columnists, a whole generation of youth are threatened with "small futures" unless we halt the downward spiral of lax values, poor motivation, and generally self-destructive behavior.

---

[3] For a complete account of how well Chapter 1 works, The National Assessment of Chapter 1 study team published their findings in three reports: Kennedy, Jung, and Orland (1986); Kennedy, Birman, and Demaline (1986); and Birman, Orland, Jung, Anson, and Garcia (1987).

The decline of youth has by now a familiar ring: It begins by decrying the pervasive scourge of drugs which in turn has lead to greater school crime and a disruptive educational climate. Learning has suffered from the erosion of academic standards, best demonstrated by the fall in test scores and the rise in dropout rates. Last, and perhaps most alarming, among poor, inner-city, minority youth, single-parents are giving birth to more and more babies. This is a tale of youth going to hell in a handbasket. Fortunately, the available data do not match this dismal view.

An Epidemic of Drugs?

The nationally representative indicators of drug and alcohol use among in-school youth are down, not up, in recent years. According to the University of Michigan's 15th national survey of high school seniors (Monitoring the Future: A Continuing Study of the Lifestyles and Values of Youth), "The longer-term trend away from the use of marijuana, cocaine and other drugs continued in 1989...the likelihood of a young person in high school or college today actively using illicit drugs is only half of what it was a decade ago" (University of Michigan, 1990).

In 1989, 20 percent of high school seniors reported using "any illicit drug within the last 30 days" compared to 37 percent in 1980. Even for "drugs of choice"—marijuana and cocaine—drug usage among high school seniors has dropped sharply since 1986. Alcohol consumption— where seniors report the highest level of abuse—has declined by one-sixth since 1980, including a 4 percent decline in 1989. In 1989, 60 percent of seniors reported having used any alcoholic beverage during the prior 30 days compared to 72 percent in 1980.

One criticism of Monitoring the Future data is that youth most prone to drug abuse may never reach their senior year. An alternative source of national data, the Federal Household Survey on Drug Abuse (National Institute on Drug Abuse [NIDA], 1989), reports similar trends. The Household Survey, based on personal interviews beginning at age 12, profiles a similar decline in the casual use of illegal drugs beginning in 1979 and accelerating from 1985 to 1988. Casual use of an illegal drug during the month prior to the interview declined 37 percent from 1985 to 1988 (National Institute of Drug Abuse, 1989).

Monitoring the Future date provide a limited glimpse at trends in drug use in urban areas. Figure 1.1 shows the trends for illicit drug use in large metropolitan communities (by the U.S. Census definition). Here again drug use has declined precipitously in recent years. In 1979, 61 percent of seniors reported using marijuana in the previous year compared with 39 percent in 1988. Similarly, 38 percent reported using "other illicit drugs" in 1981 compared to 21 percent in 1988. There's limited support for the view that drug use is more common for urban youth. Youth in large and smaller metropolitan areas reported slightly greater marijuana and "other illicit drug use" than seniors from nonmetropolitan areas.

It is important to note that despite the positive trends, the news is not all good. According to NIDA's Household Survey, addictive cocaine use has risen while causal use has declined. And based on seniors' reports of drug use, there are no drug-free schools. Setting aside marijuana use (which, according to seniors, affects virtually every school), 97 percent of all seniors attended schools where one in ten of their classmates used "other illicit drugs" during the senior year; 42 percent of seniors attended schools where one in four of their classmates had used "other illicit drugs."

Increasing School Crime?

Along with the prevalence of drugs, parents consistently cite discipline as the most worrisome school-related problem. The National Institute of Education's Safe School Study (1978) reviewed the few available studies on trends in school violence and vandalism through 1976 and concluded that:

> [The available studies] indicate an increase in assaults on teachers from 1956 to 1974, but a leveling off thereafter; an increase in robberies and assaults in the early seventies; and an increase in vandalism in the mid-sixties which leveled off around 1970 or 1971. For the offenses usually summed up in the terms violence and vandalism, the data do not give evidence that the situation is currently growing worse. (National Institute of Education, 1978, p. 35)

Keith Baker of the Office of Planning, Budget, and Evaluation, for the U.S. Department of Education, reached the following conclusion from the data between 1976 and 1985:

> The picture is confusing. There have been increases in the incidence of some crimes—most notably crimes against teachers—and declines in the incidence of other crimes—most notably thefts against students. On balance, the data suggest a slight overall improvement. (Baker, 1985, p. 485)

Figure 1.1.

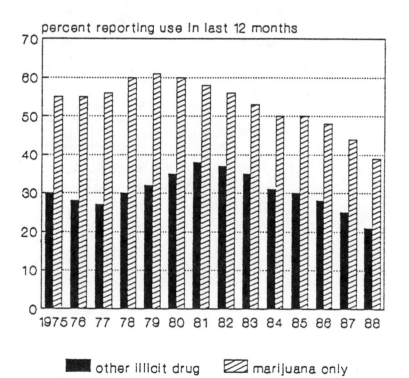

Trends in Illicit Drug Use
Among High School Seniors
in Large Metropolitan Areas

percent reporting use in last 12 months

other illicit drug   marijuana only

Johnston, O'Malley and Backman, 1989
National Institute on Drug Abuse

The best trend data on student victimization are available through the National Crime Survey of the U.S. Department of Justice. Since many crimes and incidents of misconduct in school are not reported to teachers and principals, these survey data provide in some regards a more complete picture of misbehavior than school administration records. The Justice Department data do not report "victimless" crimes like narcotics violations or the possession of weapons. Figure 1.2 shows curves which were fitted to the annual data between 1973 and 1987 on attempted assaults, robberies, and thefts within secondary schools. Over this period the rate of assaults showed considerable year-to-year fluctuations without a clear-cut trend. The likelihood of being victimized through robbery or theft appears to decline after 1980 for both robberies and thefts, but these changes are not statistically significant. Based on data not reported here, similar patterns were found among completed assault, robbery, and theft rates over the same years (Moles, 1989).

Figure 1.2.

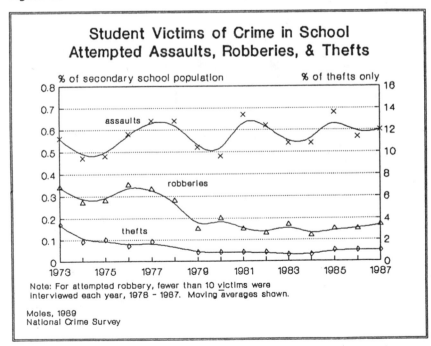

Student Victims of Crime in School
Attempted Assaults, Robberies, & Thefts

Note: For attempted robbery, fewer than 10 victims were interviewed each year, 1978 - 1987. Moving averages shown.

Moles, 1989
National Crime Survey

The evidence that in-school misbehavior is no worse, and perhaps slightly better, is corroborated by the perceptions of teachers and school administrators. When asked if classroom disruption had improved or worsened between 1980–81 and 1985–86, 63 percent of high school teachers and 88 percent of school administrators believed that classrooms were either less disruptive or no more disruptive than five years earlier (Office of Educational Research and Improvement, 1988).

If, as Baker suggest, school safety may have improved slightly, several points should be emphasized. First, accurate crime-related statistics are exceedingly difficult to collect and undercounts are always possible. Second, these data only extend to 1987; according to FBI crime reports the overall crime rate—which is correlated with the school crime rate—has risen since 1984 (Gottfredson & Hirschi, 1989). Third, most of the crime-related statistics show considerable year-to-year variations while net changes have been small. Last, from a policymaker's perspective, over time shifts in the amount of student misbehavior are less important than the fact that it exists at all. The main victim of student misbehavior is learning. Beyond some threshold—which social scientists have yet to explore—learning slows to a crawl if the teacher must struggle to maintain a semblance of order.

Are students who attend urban schools or schools in disadvantaged neighborhoods more likely to report school crime and school discipline problems? Data obtained from a survey of secondary school principals in 1985 (collected by the National Center for Education Statistics) show that rate at which students are caught selling illegal drugs at school and the rate at which law violations are reported to police varies directly with both the poverty-level of the school's student body and whether the school is in an urban setting or not (Figures 1.3 and 1.4). The likelihood of a student reporting the theft of a personal item (over $10 in value) is also more likely in a high-poverty school.

An Erosion of Standards?

According to the American Council of Education (El-Khawas, 1989), high school grades awarded to college-bound students have not risen overall since 1980.[4] More significantly, two national studies of student transcripts—High School and Beyond (transcripts for 1982 graduates)

---

[4] These data, collected annually by the American Council of Education, do not represent a true sample of institutions of higher education or a true sample of incoming college freshmen.

Figure 1.3.

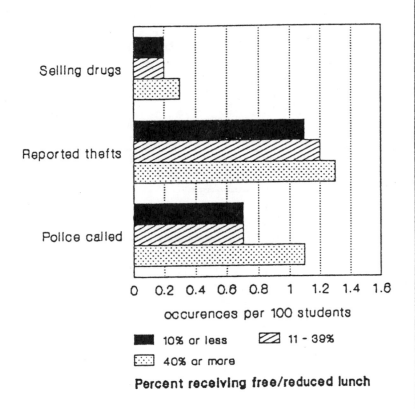

Student Infractions in High School
By Percent of Students Receiving
Free or Reduced Lunch, 1985

Figure 1.4.

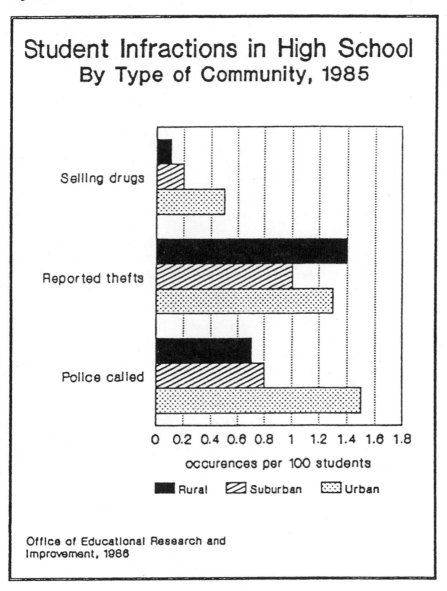

Student Infractions in High School
By Type of Community, 1985

Office of Educational Research and
Improvement, 1986

and the High School Transcript Study (transcripts for 1987 graduates)—show substantial gains in the number of academic courses
taken by the graduating class of 1987 as contrasted with the class of
1982. As summarized by the Educational Testing Service [ETS]:

> Increases in mathematics course-taking were substantial for all racial
> ethnic groups, and in some cases, dramatic...In the sciences, course-
> taking gains were registered for all racial/ethnic groups, although the
> point gains were generally more modest for physics than for other
> subjects. (ETS, 1989, p. 6)

State efforts to raise high school graduation requirements have had an
uncertain effect on academic course taking. Data collected from the
college-bound students who took the SAT exams in 1975, 1982, and
1988 show small increases before 1982 in the number courses taken in
English, mathematics, and social studies (ETS, p. 8), but many of the
reform efforts to raise course-taking requirements were also underway before 1982.

Despite steady improvements, minorities and blacks receive educational programs and offerings that differ in kind and substance from
those of white students. Black students are more likely to be enrolled
in special education programs and vocational education programs.
And college-bound black students compared to white students take
fewer semesters of mathematics, physical sciences, and social studies.
Within subject areas black students are exposed to less challenging
educational offerings which, in turn, are less likely to enhance the
development of higher order cognitive skills (College Entrance Examination Board, 1985).

Declining Test Scores?

The perception that test scores have dropped sharply since 1967 is
based on the lower performance of college-bound seniors who sign up
each year to take the SAT or ACT college admissions examinations. A
look at the National Assessment of Educational Progress (NAEP)
reports since 1969 paints a more balanced picture (Applebee, Langer,
& Mullis, 1989; Mullis & Jenkins, 1990). These data show that all
youth read and compute better now than in the early 1970s, and
particularly encouraging are the advances black youth have made in
math and reading performance.

Figure 1.5 shows the performance of 9-, 13-, and 17-year-olds in
assessments of reading and mathematics proficiency at various years.

Figure 1.5.

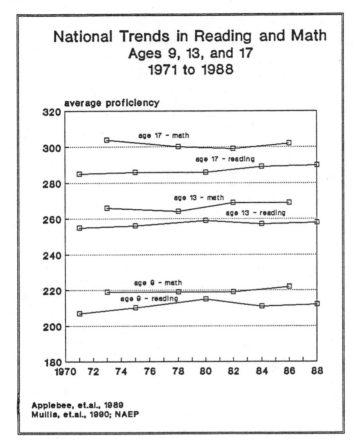

National Trends in Reading and Math
Ages 9, 13, and 17
1971 to 1988

Applebee, et.al., 1989
Mullis, et.al., 1990; NAEP

At 9 and 17, students were reading significantly better in 1988 than in 1971. In mathematics, 9- and 13-year-olds over time became more proficient, while 17-year-olds recovered most of their earlier losses. However, in science 17-year-olds lost substantial ground (see Figure 1.6), while the recent gains of 13-year-olds barely compensated for earlier loses and 9-year-olds failed to catch up.

Overall the strongest gains in mathematics and reading test scores were registered by young black students, particularly those from urban, disadvantaged communities and from the southeastern states (College Entrance Examination Board, 1985). Nearly 30 percent of

Figure 1.6.

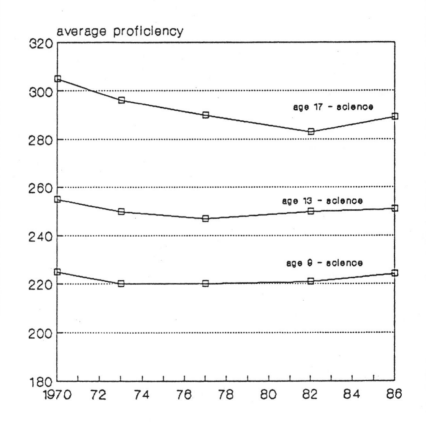

National Trends in Science Skills
Ages 9, 13, and 17
1970 to 1986

Applebee, Langer, and Mullis, 1989
NAEP, Educational Testing Service

9-year-old black students failed in 1971 to demonstrate rudimentary skills in reading. By 1988, this number has fallen to 14 percent. In addition to gains in rudimentary skills, the number of Advanced Placement exams on which minority students achieved passing grades more than doubled between 1984 and 1988 (Office of Planning, Budget and Evaluation, 1989).

Figure 1.7 shows over time shifts in the average difference for reading and mathematics proficiency between white and black students. The gap in white/black performances in reading and mathematics declined steadily from 1971 to 1988. With the exception of a four-year plateau (from 1980 to 1984) in the mean reading proficiency difference between 9-year-old blacks and 9-year-old whites, the trend lines from 1972 to 1988 are significant for all ages in both reading and math performances. Looking at the NAEP data for the 1970s, Burton and Jones (1984, p. 14) drew the following conclusion: "When achievement for white students has declined, that for black students has declined less; when whites have improved, blacks have improved more." These patterns have held through the 1980s. Since 1971, the overall reading proficiency gap between black students and white students has narrowed roughly by half.[5]

Escalating Dropout Rates?

Trends in dropout rates for grades 10 to 12 according to the Current Population Survey (U.S. Department of Commerce, Bureau of the Census) for the population as a whole and for subgroups of whites and blacks have fallen since 1979. Figure 1.8 shows the percent of dropouts among black youth in particular has fallen since 1970. For Hispanics there is no consistent trend in dropout rates over the past 15 years. White males during the middle-to-late 1970s experienced a slight rise in dropping out, which has since been followed by slight, but steady improvements (Frase, 1989).

---

[5] The reading performance differences between blacks and whites declined between 1971 to 1988 by 15 points (on NAEP's proficiency scale) for 17-year-olds, by 20 points for 13-year-olds, and by 33 points for 9-year-olds. This reduced the overall black–white performance "gap" in reading by 33 percent (14.6/43.8), 52 percent (20.1/38.5), and 62 percent (32.5/52.8) respectively for the three age groups. Averaging across the three age groups, black–white differences in reading have declined roughly by half (49 percent) over the last 20 years.

Figure 1.7.

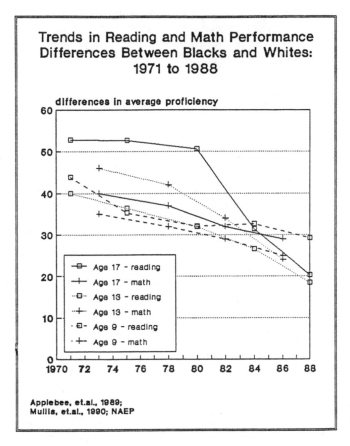

Despite the improvements, dropout rates are high for blacks and especially Hispanic youth from low socioeconomic status families and for those in single-parent families (Frase, 1989). Dropout rates in some urban areas have been estimated to exceed the national averages by three or four times (Sherman, 1987). The disparity between steadily improving national figures and the accelerating dropout rates reported in most major cities may be explained in part by the increasing concentration of poverty in central-city neighborhoods.

To test this hypothesis with Census data, Figure 1.9 compares the total school enrollment status of 18- to 21-year-old whites, blacks, and central-city blacks in 1975 and 1986. Consistent with the earlier dropout trends, blacks have made significant strides toward completing secondary school in the last 10 years. These data, though, show

Figure 1.8.

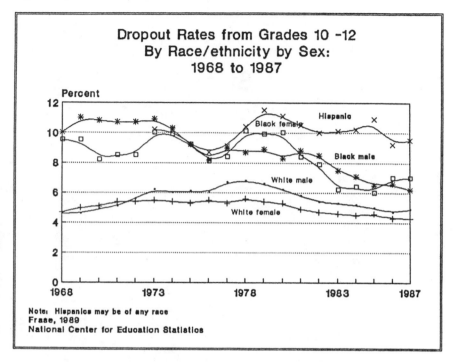

Dropout Rates from Grades 10 -12 By Race/ethnicity by Sex: 1968 to 1987

Note: Hispanics may be of any race
Frase, 1989
National Center for Education Statistics

that little progress has been made in access to college. Whites again have maintained stable levels of school attainment with some improvement in college enrollments. Inner-city blacks show a remarkable degree of similarity to blacks overall in their enrollment status at all levels of education.

Figure 1.10 shows the enrollment status in 1986 of 18- to 24-year-olds for all races and for blacks by family income.[6] For all races, family income is closely linked to educational attainment. Among families with an income below $10,000, a surprising number of overage students are still enrolled in high school or perhaps a high school equivalency program. Among blacks with a family income under $10,000, these data show the dropout rate for 18- to 24-year-olds

---

[6] Since family income is meant to indicate the socioeconomic background of youth, the CPS income data should be interpreted wtih caution. Some dropouts—though poverty-stricken—may be living independently. In those instances family income may reflect a consequence rather than a precondition of dropping out.

Figure 1.9.

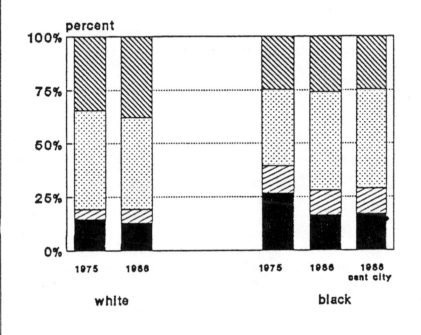

Enrollment Status of Persons
18 to 21 Years old by Race:
October 1975, 1986

Figure 1.10.

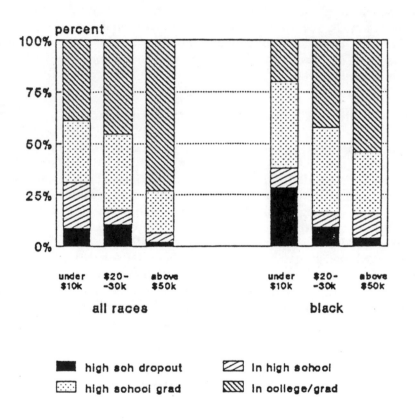

Enrollment Status of Persons 18 to 24 Years old by Race and Family Income∗: October 1986

Legend:
- high sch dropout
- high school grad
- in high school
- in college/grad

all races: under $10k, $20-30k, above $50k

black: under $10k, $20-30k, above $50k

U.S. Department of Commerce, 1988, 1989
∗excludes persons married-spouse present

exceeds 28 percent with another 9.2 percent still enrolled in some form of a secondary school program. The enrollment status of families in the middle-range income class ($20,000 to $30,000) is similar between blacks and all races. Black families in the upper-income levels have many fewer youth enrolled in college.

These data provide some support for the view that dropout rates in particular neighborhoods—those with increasing concentrations of very poor, black families whether in urban, suburban, or rural settings—may be several times greater than the national average for whites overall, for blacks overall, or even for all blacks living in urban areas. Even if blacks reach parity with whites in less than one generation (16 years as forecasted by the National Urban League in their 1989 report, "Stalling Out: The Relative Progress of African Americans"), there may still be very poor neighborhoods with very high dropout rates.

More Births to Unmarried, Minority Teenagers?

Perhaps the most alarming statistics of all are related to "children having children." As Figure 1.11 shows, the rate of birth to unmarried women is especially high among black teenagers, but the number of births per 100 unmarried black women 15 to 24 years old has declined since 1970. Among unmarried white teenagers, the rate of birth has steadily risen since 1965.[7] A related but different statistic, the proportion of children living in single-parent families, has grown for black families because divorce rates have risen and fertility rates among married black women have fallen. In 1970, 20 percent of all black households were headed by a single parent. In 1985, single-parent families were 31 percent of all black households (Office of Educational Research and Improvement, 1988, p. 16).

ARE THE PROBLEMS OF DISADVANTAGED YOUTH OR IS THE PROBLEM OF DISADVANTAGED YOUTH CAUSING ALARM?

These data suggest several conclusions. First, there have been significant improvements over time in lowering the at-risk behavior of youth generally, and most improvements have been sustained for over a

---

[7] The census category for "black" includes women from "black and other non-white racial groups."

Figure 1.11.

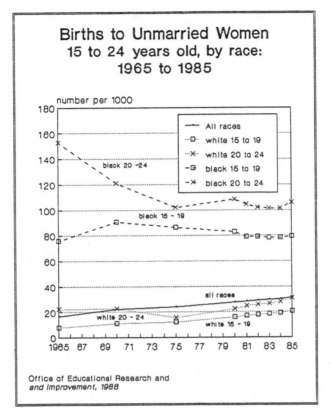

**Births to Unmarried Women
15 to 24 years old, by race:
1965 to 1985**

number per 1000

Legend:
— All races
··□·· white 15 to 19
···×·· white 20 to 24
−□ black 15 to 19
−× black 20 to 24

Office of Educational Research and
and Improvement, 1988

decade—before the educational excellence movement got underway. Second, the available data for identifying educational performance trends among black youth have shown steady improvements in academic course taking, school attainment, and school achievement. (Though performance gaps between racial and ethnic groups were not described in this chapter, sizable differences in school performances still separate blacks, whites, and Hispanics.) Third, even as the overall trends for high school completion looks promising, low-income, minority youth are dramatically less likely to make satisfactory progress toward school completion. Without adequate data, we do not know if the school-related prospects for youth who face compounded disadvantages or who are associated with several at-risk factors have improved over time, as they have for youth overall.

The positive direction of these data raises a new issue. If both majority and minority youth have shown improvements over the last 10 years in education and education-related outcomes, what explains the intense concern that a "national crisis" threatens the economic and social well-being of today's youth? One hypothesis is that deepening poverty and isolation for minority youth in ghetto neighborhoods threatens a significant number of youth which the nationally representative databases—such as the U.S. Census' Current Population Survey—are simply not capturing. Another view is that despite the improved educational prospects for disadvantaged students overall, the increased *number* of disadvantaged students poses new challenges.

The Underclass Hypothesis

Is there evidence that the symptoms of disadvantagement—joblessness, crime, school failure, and teenage motherhood—have grown faster in poor inner-city neighborhoods than elsewhere? A review of those data extends beyond this chapter, but recent studies have debated whether isolated neighborhoods are really exhibiting new trends or old patterns. It seems clear that joblessness—which some believe to be the central issue—has worsened over the last 20 years. Hughes (1989) investigated changes in the geographic concentration of chronic joblessness in eight major cities to find that the fraction of men over the age of 16 who worked less than half the year rose from 26 percent in 1969 to 39 percent in 1979. But according to Jencks (1989), increased joblessness has affected all social strata making joblessness today no more limited to either "race or place" than a generation ago.

For education policy, the debate over demographic and economic forces affecting inner-city neighborhoods matters if neighborhoods affect children's learning. There is tentative evidence that it does. According to a literature review by Mayer and Jencks (1989), the average socioeconomic level of a pupil's elementary school may have a sizable effect on how much students learn, although the available research is weak. The socioeconomic composition of high schools, on the other hand, appears to have a small effect on how much the average high school student learns. Attending high school with classmates from better neighborhoods appears to increase a student's prospects for staying in school, although attending an affluent high school provides a negligible advantage for attending or graduating from college.

The Minority-Majority Hypothesis

In 1985, Harold Hodgkinson urged educators to prepare for the growing number of educationally disadvantaged students "who will be poorer, more ethnically and linguistically diverse, and who will have more handicaps that will affect their learning." This perspective is consistent with the trends for disadvantaged youth reported here. It does not suggest that disadvantaged students are worse off today but, as Pallas, Natriello, and McDill (1989) have written:

> [T]he size of the disadvantaged population will assume an unprecedented proportions in the coming years. Failure to anticipate the coming changes in the composition of the student population and to plan appropriate responses will leave us not with the same educational problems we face today, but perhaps with problems so severe and widespread as to threaten our economic welfare and even our social and political stability. (p. 21)

Both hypotheses touch upon vital concerns for policymakers. At least two issues remain. First, overall estimates of the size of the educationally disadvantaged population are generally around one quarter to one third of the total student population. Pallas, Natriello, and McDill, for example, argue that "even conservative estimate put the proportion of educationally disadvantaged students at one third." It may be that a much smaller group of students, those who suffer from the cumulative disadvantages of overlapping risk factors such as growing up in a poor, single-parent family inside an inner-city neighborhood, may experience a qualitatively more potent set of obstacles to academic success. Their educational prospects may be declining dramatically—though we don't have adequate data to explore this—even as the larger part of the disadvantaged one-third are making small, but steady educational gains.

Second, more disadvantaged youth in the classroom does not mean that schools in high-poverty neighborhoods cannot succeed or that urban schools are doomed to fail unless they are radically reformed. These data indicate that disadvantaged students have made academic gains over the last few years. But, as more disadvantaged students enter the educational system, more services and greater support will be needed to maintain the positive trends in school achievement and attainment. To accelerate the gains of disadvantaged youth and seriously attack the large performance gaps between racial, ethnic, and socioeconomic groups will require leaps in instructional efficiency or more targeted resources or both. Either way relies on a tightly focused view of whom to help and how.

REFERENCES

Applebee, A.N., Langer, J.A., & Mullis, I.V.S. (1989). *Crossroads in American education: A summary of findings*. Princeton, NJ: National Assessment of Educational Progress.

Ascher, C. (1987). *Chapter 1 programs: New guides from the research*. New York: ERIC Clearinghouse on Urban Education.

Baker, K. (1985, March). Research evidence of a school discipline problem. *Phi Delta Kappan*, pp. 482-496.

Bereiter, C. (1985, April). The changing face of educational disadvantagement. *Phi Delta Kappan*, pp. 538-541.

Birman, B.F., Orland, M.E., Jung, R.K., Anson, R.J., & Garcia, G.N. (1987). *The current operation of the Chapter 1 program*. Washington, DC: U.S. Government Printing Office.

Bureau of the Census. (1984). America's Black population: 1970 to 1982—A statistical view. In J.D. Williams (Eds.), *The state of Black America, 1984* (pp. 171-181). New York: National Urban League.

Burton, N.W., & Jones, L.V. (1982, April). Recent trends in achievement levels of Black and White youth. *Educational Researcher*, pp. 10-14, 17.

Carter, L.F. (1983). *A study of compensatory and elementary education: The sustaining effects study*. Menlo Park, CA: System Development Corporation.

Carter, L.F. (1984). The sustaining effects of compensatory and elementary education. *Educational Researcher, 13*, 4-13.

College Entrance Examination Board. (1985). *Equality and excellence: The educational status of Black Americans*. New York: College Board Publications.

Educational Testing Service. (1989). *What Americans study*. Princeton, NJ: Educational Testing Service Publications.

El-Khawas, E. (1989). *Campus trends, 1988*. Washington, DC: American Council of Education.

Ellwood, D.T. (1988). *Poor support: Poverty in the American family*. New York: Basic Books.

Frase, M. (1989). *Dropout rates in the United States: 1988*. Washington, DC: U.S. Department of Education, National Center for Education Statistics.

Gottfredson, M., & Hirschi, T. (1989, September 10). Why we're losing the war on crime. *Washington Post*, p. C3.

Hodgkinson, H. (1985). *All one system: Demographics of education, kindergarten through graduate school*. Washington, DC: Institute for Educational Leadership.

Hughes, M.A. (1989). *Poverty in cities*. Washington, DC: National League of Cities.

Jencks, C. (1989). What is the underclass—and is it growing? *Focus, 12,* 14-26.

Johnston, L.D., O'Malley, P.M., & Backman, J.G. (1989). *Drug use, drinking, and smoking: National survey results from high school, college, and young adult populations 1975–1988.* Rockville, MD: National Institute on Drug Abuse.

Kennedy, M.M., Birman, B.F., & Demaline, R. (1986). *The effectiveness of Chapter 1 services.* Washington, DC: U.S. Government Printing Office.

Kennedy, M.M., Jung, R.K., & Orland, M.E. (1986). *Poverty, achievement and the distribution of compensatory education services.* Washington, DC: U.S. Government Printing Office.

Mayer, S.E., & Jencks, C. (1989, March). Growing up in poor neighborhoods: How much does it matter? *Science,* pp. 1441-1445.

Moles, O.C. (1989). *Trends in student misconduct: The 70s and 80s.* Unpublished manuscript, Office of Educational Research and Improvement, Washington, DC.

Mullis, I.V.S., & Jenkins, L.B. (1990). *The reading report card, 1971–88: Trends from the nation's report card.* Princeton, NJ: National Assessment of Educational Progress.

National Institute of Education. (1978). *Violent schools—Safe schools: The Safe School Study Report to the Congress, Vol. I.* Washington, DC: U.S. Government Printing Office.

National Institute on Drug Abuse. (1989). *National Household Survey on Drug Abuse: 1988 Population Estimates* (DHHS Publication No. (ADM) 89-1636). Washington, DC: U.S. Government Printing Office.

National Urban League. (1989). *Stalling out: The relative progress of African Americans.* Washington, DC: Author.

Office of Educational Research and Improvement. (1986). *Discipline in public secondary schools. OERI Bulletin.* Washington, DC: Center for Education Statistics.

Office of Educational Research and Improvement. (1988). *Youth indicators, 1988: Trends in the well-being of American youth.* Washington, DC: Government Printing Office.

Office of Planning, Budget and Evaluation. (1989). *The disadvantaged population.* Unpublished briefing paper. Washington, DC: U.S. Department of Education.

Orshansky, M. (1965, July). Counting the poor: Another look at the poverty profile. *Social Security Bulletin.*

Pallas, A.M., Natriello, G., & McDill, E.L. (1989, June). The changing nature of the disadvantaged population: Current dimensions and future trends. *Educational Researcher,* pp. 16-22.

Ralph, J. (1989, January). Improving education for the disadvantaged: Do we know whom to help? *Phi Delta Kappan,* pp. 395-401.

Ralph, J., & Dwyer, M.C. (1988). *Making the case: Evidence of program effectiveness in schools and classrooms.* Washington, DC: Government Printing Office.

Rowan, B., & Guthrie, L.F. (1989). The quality of Chapter 1 instruction: Results from a study of twenty-four schools. In R.E. Slavin, N.L. Karweit, & N.A.

Madden (Eds.), *Effective programs for students at risk* (pp. 195-220). Boston: Allyn and Bacon.

Sherman, J. (1987). *Dropping out of school: Volume I: Causes and consequences for male and female youth.* Washington, DC: Pelavin Associates.

University of Michigan [press release]. (1990, February 9). *Teen drug use continues to decline, according to U-M survey; cocaine down for third straight year.* Ann Arbor, MI: News and Information Services.

U.S. Department of Commerce, Bureau of the Census. (1988, 1989, October). School enrollment—Social and economic characteristics of students. *Current Population Reports* (Series P-20). Washington, DC: Government Printing Office.

2
Implementing Programs and Policies for Young Children and Their Families: Who Is Responsible?

Sharon L. Kagan

Taking a historical perspective on the development of child care and early education programs indicates that intensive expansion has been occasioned by broadly felt societal needs. Major efforts, launched by federal impetus, have proliferated at turbulent times in our national history. The Lanham Act, which provided thousands of day care slots, was enacted in response to the crisis of World War II and the need to employ many women for the war effort. Though the act provided the foundation for a promising infrastructure for early childhood services, it was never realized because federal support was withdrawn following the war. In the 1960s, the "war on poverty" brought another wave of federal support for young children's services, including the nation's Head Start program. Additional services were later added as the government emphasized its commitment to young children and their families through the creation of a national laboratory for early childhood education (Zigler, 1979). Through the federal Office of Child Development (now the Administration for Children, Youth and Families), many new approaches were researched and new programs were mounted. Conversely, in the late 1970s and early 1980s, when child care and early education were not yet seen as a social panacea to intransigent problems (e.g., illiteracy, school dropout, teen pregnancy),

29

direct federal support for programs did not expand. In essence, then, the history of federal involvement in the care and education of young children has represented a tide, ebbing and flowing in response to the pull of societal need and national circumstances.

Attention accorded the field of early education in the late 1980s by the media, foundations, legislative groups, academicians, and the National Governors' Association (1987), the Council of Chief State School Officers (1988), and major business and industry (Committee for Economic Development, (CED), 1987) indicates that the care and education of young children has once again become a major public policy concern, transcending governmental or social welfare orientations. That issues related to young children have been promoted to the front pages of our major national presses and that 26 states have enacted legislation enhancing services to young children and their families (Marx & Seligson, 1988) are welcome events, demonstrating the extent of national concern. What has precipitated this current interest in and growth of early childhood and child development programs? How do these initiatives relate to past policy efforts? And what light do they shed on future policy efforts on behalf of at-risk children and families?

A review of recent policy initiatives, this chapter suggests that the late 1980s have stimulated activity and have added considerable services to the social landscape, but that these early education initiatives merely create the illusion of reform. New efforts have not yet altered the way we care for and educate young children, particularly at-risk children, so that many of the problems with which the field has long been confronted remain unchanged. Although recognizing the challenges, the initiatives of the 1980s have done little to reshape the nation's episodic and piecemeal approach to policy for children and families or to address the basic problem of fragmented and inequitable service delivery.

EARLY EDUCATION IN THE 1980S

The government's role in early childhood programs and policies seesawed in the 1980s. The early years of the decade were characterized by a "New Federalism." Advocating a divestiture of responsibility for early childhood issues from the federal government to the private sector and the states, the New Federalism of the early 1980s called for decentralization, privatization, and deregulation of many services. For example, in the case of early care and education, the federal government relinquished its role in setting standards to the point that the Reagan Administration went on record as opposing any sort of governmental regulation of child care (Kahn & Kamerman, 1987). At the local level, these changes forced many programs to close or to modify their ways of operating. Some were able to link with other providers, and some sought and received foundation support. Corporate support reached an all-time high and saved many endangered programs, but was insufficient to meet the need created by the withdrawal of federal support. For example, in 1988, it was estimated that only 3,300 of the nation's 6 million employers provided any help to meet their employees' child care needs (Friedman, 1988).

As federal services were jeopardized and related needs emerged, new and strengthened advocacy efforts took root. Several important committees related to children and families were established in the U.S. Congress. Academicians, becoming more aware of the implications of their research findings for policy formation, testified before these newly created committees and disseminated their research findings to the public. The timing was propitious: A spate of research reports from longitudinal studies proclaimed the importance of early intervention, and contributed an empirical rationale to the need for programmatic expansion (Berrueta-Clement, Schweinhart, Barnett, Epstein, & Weikart, 1984; Lazar & Darlington, 1982) that was occasioned by federal cutbacks.

Simultaneously, public concern about the early experiences of children was strengthened by rapidly changing demographic trends. The rise in divorce rates, single-parent families, children in poverty, and mothers joining the out-of-home workforce all contributed to the push for stronger, more comprehensive child and family policies.

Given the extensive media coverage afforded these issues, by the mid-1980s, early childhood programs took on a different role: They were advanced as one answer to the nation's deep-seated social problems. Even though the number of three- and four-year-old children receiving services tripled between 1965 and 1985 (from 11% to 39%) according to the U.S. Department of Education (1986), a press for more services took root. Many services expanded as a result of *state* legislative initiatives, a particularly striking fact in view of the states' historical record of uninvolvement with preschool education. Before 1984, only two states (California and New York) contributed over $3 million in state funds to programs for young children (Grubb, 1986). By the mid- to late-1980s, however, more than 20 states had joined this list (Blank & Wilkins, 1985; Kagan, 1985; Marx & Seligson, 1988; Schweinhart, 1985; Weil, 1986).

In several states—Texas, South Carolina, and Massachusetts— these early childhood initiatives were launched as a part of broad educational reform. In others, expansion of early childhood programs was closely linked with existing programs or funding streams. In

Maine, for example, part of the expansion took the form of increasing, at state expense, the number of slots available in Head Start. Most other state efforts were funded through departments of education at the state level, although in a few cases, expansion efforts were integrated with ongoing efforts administered through state departments of community affairs or social services.

Taken together, these trends indicate that the 1980s initiatives are different from those of the 1940s and the 1960s. We have seen that services emerged from state rather than federal initiative. In addition, acknowledging thoughtful, scholarly work over the past 20 years recognizing that young children's growth and development is best nurtured within the context of family and community (Bronfenbrenner, 1979), the new initiatives mouth a commitment to holistic services (health, mental health, nutrition, social work, speech, and psychological services) that was seen previously only in a few efforts (e.g., Head Start, New York State Experimental Pre-Kindergarten Program). Unfortunately, only a few of the newer programs actually provide funds for such services.

Similarly, while research has clearly demonstrated the importance of parent involvement and staff development, only a limited number of the 1980s initiatives fund these services, in spite of a rhetorical commitment to them. Decidedly reflective of the era in which they were mounted, the state-initiated 1980s efforts emphasize cost-effectiveness. A call for linking and networking characterizes the new efforts with the goal of capitalizing on extant community services and minimizing duplication of effort. Routinely, in these new efforts ancillary services are provided *through*, not *by*, the program.

The Problem of Fragmentation

Although the 1980s initiatives differ substantially from those of previous decades, they do reflect a pattern set by earlier efforts in that they have been mounted as a response to near-crisis conditions. Consequently, such initiatives are often created as new and separate entities, often never fully meshing with existing services or systems. While seeming to ameliorate the existing crisis (in this case a need for more slots for children), such short-sighted approaches not only sidestep, but exacerbate, the systemic, long-term problems. In this respect, the initiatives of the 1980s have added to the serious lack of a cohesive infrastructure in early childhood policies.

A verbalized commitment to partnerships seems to contradict this stance. Yet, when investigated, it is clear that the commitment to partnerships has not gone far enough. With initiatives in New York

City, Washington, Florida, Ohio, and Massachusetts representing exceptions, the 1980s efforts placed priority on increasing the number of children in service without a commensurate emphasis on creating partnerships to eradicate the problems of accessibility and fragmentation. Few efforts have engaged day care providers, Head Start, and the public schools in collaborative efforts to serve young children, whether it be the siting of programs or common training. Hence, under the guise of educational reform and with dramatic fanfare from the press, the 1980s efforts give the illusion of a fresh new approach. In reality, most programs have not offered comprehensive services, intensive training, special resources to meet the needs of families, or demonstrated a significant commitment to alter the inequity and fragmentation that characterize the field.

Child Care vs. Education

A second serious problem is that most of the 1980s efforts perpetuate the division between care and education for young children that has characterized the field for decades.

One conception of child care emanates from a social welfare orientation to provide support for parents who work or attend school. Child care as viewed from this perspective (and federally subsidized child care, in particular) has typically been thought of as custodial care. In contrast to this social welfare orientation which focused on the needs of adults and society, child-centered services were established in different sectors with the primary goal of benefiting children. Some programs, established by or at the urging of middle-class parents, largely through the voluntary sector, provided opportunities for children to play and socialize. Other programs, like Head Start and Title I/Chapter 1 of ESEA/ECIA for low-income youngsters, were mounted at federal initiative and focused on providing comprehensive services and opportunities to enhance children's cognitive skills and social competence.

The implications of the historical legacy of divergent funding streams in early care and education are manifest in a host of policy and practical issues. There is, for example, no clearly defined federal agency or legislative committee that has sole responsibility for early care and education programs. Because program jurisdiction is lodged in education, health, labor, and human agency committees, early care and education lacked, until recently, policymaking muscle to move so many diverse groups and agendas. Even now, with the expansion of early childhood services, it is interesting to note that the majority of efforts build upon the existing service delineations and are funded as attachments either to education or human services. While the split is recognized in the policy arena, and national organizations have been funded to help selected states overcome this dichotomy, there has been only limited success in arresting the care/education split at the policy level.

The care/education split also has important equity implications in the areas of occupational status and salary parity. Not only do early childhood professionals, most of whom are women, earn less than the average salary of men and less than care providers for other service industries, but there is serious intrafield inequity based on the care/ education split. The perceived difference between "teachers" and "caregivers" are manifest in their training requirements as well as in their wages and benefits. Teachers working in early childhood settings in public schools may earn twice the salary and receive significantly greater benefits than child care workers in settings virtually across the street, but which are under the institutional aegis of child care or Head Start. Parity is absent not only between education and child care, but within each community. For example, within one funding stream, the government, vast discrepancies exist in the amount of training and salaries provided. The federal government, as represented in a U.S. Department of Labor publication (1977), sanctions and perpetuates this split by describing the duties of caregivers as custodial (e.g., helping children with dressing, toileting) and those of early childhood teachers as formally educational (e.g., planning group activities to stimulate learning and social growth).

Unfortunately, the wave of early childhood initiatives that has been launched to date, with several notable exceptions, has not fully addressed the care/education dichotomy. This 1980s cohort of new programs can best be characterized as the accommodation cohort. When agencies are asked to link, to collaborate, and to plan with providers of services in private and public agencies, they often lack the funding or the administrative clout needed to support active collaboration. What is intended as partnership is generally reduced to polite accommodation.

The Problem of Equity

No less serious than concerns emanating from the care/education split are those centered on how this nation plans to ensure access to services for preschool children in an equitable way. It is clear that preschool programs in the United States are not available to all children equally. Head Start, for example, now reaches about 16 percent of the children who need its services (Children's Defense Fund, (CDF), 1988). As significantly, the (non)system dramatically segregates children by income. Poor children are usually enrolled in subsidized programs, while middle- and upper-class youngsters attend fee-based programs. Even ardent champions of high quality Head Start and Head Start-like programs recognize that the economic segregation of children is a critical program weakness (Zigler, 1986).

Economic segregation of children is troublesome on several counts. First, it flies in the face of research that indicates the positive effects of desegregation (Crain & Mahard, 1978; Hawley, 1981; Weinberg, 1975). Second, it represents a blatant violation of the law of the land which mandates integration (*Brown v. Board of Education*, 1954). If serving all children, and serving them together, once they reach age five, is mandated, how can we rationalize segregating children who may be just a year younger? To what extent does the social stratification we have allowed to persist in early childhood perpetuate class inequities? How can this dilemma be resolved? The early childhood community must grapple with these hard questions. By condoning a two-tier system of programs for young children, the nation is approving a system of social and economic segregation. To date, there have been scattered attempts to provide prekindergarten services to economically integrated populations. While some programs (e.g., Head Start) allow for 10 percent over-income enrollment, few programs take advantage of this proviso because of their desire to serve the most needy youngsters first. Within the wave of the 1980s programs, few, if any, have even begun to address this issue. The Giant Step effort (Cohen, 1986) in New York City called for universal services, but served primarily high-needs children and their families.

Even if the access question were addressed, and programs were made universally available to all families who want them, would the problem be solved? Universality itself raises other concerns: Will a universal approach to early education expand opportunities for low-income youngsters, or will limited funding mean that in the name of integration, slots previously assigned to low-income youth will be allocated to middle- and upper-class children? Does the *provision* of universal services mean *utilization* of services universally? And finally, given extant (and largely segregated) housing patterns, how will universality address the integration of youngsters across income levels in any meaningful way? Answers to these questions are remote, indeed. In fact, only recently have we as a cadre of professionals raised these seemingly insolvable issues.

While the nation is blessed with a groundswell of commitment to young children and their families, too little effort has been expended to redress the fundamental issues of the early childhood/child development field. Problems—fragmentation, care vs. education, inequity—

will continue to escalate unless principles are developed to guide well-intentioned policymakers as they craft child and family policy.

THE MYTH AND REALITY OF EARLY
EDUCATION POLICY

Debate about what constitutes child and family policy in the United States is as widespread as our definitions of family itself. While scholars generally agree that there is still no such thing as a coherent family policy in our country (Bane, 1978; Steiner, 1981), they vary in the way they label policy. For example, Kamerman and Kahn (1978) advocate a broad definition that embraces "everything that government does to and for the family." Others (Johnson et al., 1978) equate policy with "family-relevant programs, maintained by the government," citing the very existence of such programs as evidence of a de facto family policy. Moroney (1979) and others argue that because there is no well-articulated policy, programs generated are often at cross-purposes with one another, contradictory and counterproductive. This line of reasoning supports the position of those who interpret the lack of a stated policy to be in itself a policy of neglect (Kagan, Klugman, & Zigler, 1983; Marmor, 1983). Finally, others claim that we are too pluralistic a society for any comprehensive policy to be effective: that the vastness of the United States and the diversity of values and behaviors regarding family life enables policymakers to do little more than acknowledge concern for the family (Barbaro, 1979; Feldman, 1979).

Out of this diversity of definitions and viewpoints, many have called for the development of a "more systematic and responsible approach to family problems" (Dempsy, 1981, p. 38). Moynihan (1965), over 25 years ago, indicated:

> A national family policy need only declare that it is the policy of the American government to promote the stability and well-being of the American family: that social programs of the federal government will be formulated and administered with this object in mind. (p. 283)

Calls for attention to the family emanate not only from liberals, but from conservatives whose "pro-family" agenda swept the nation, further piquing public attention and broadening the range of issues and options. Why are there so many difficulties in achieving a consensus on child and family policy in the United States, and what are the consequences, for young children in particular?

The challenge of creating family policy in the United States is embedded in the ideology that gave birth to this nation—the primacy of the individual over state, and the nonintervention of the government into private (read family) affairs. Scholars have pointed out that in our constitution, the word "family" never appears (Moynihan, 1965). U.S. tradition focused on the individual, and indeed the mythology of success, best personified by Horatio Alger, focuses on the success of the individual. It is the individual who is responsible for his or her own success and well-being. The family was construed as an extension of the self, not the state. It, too, functioned autonomously, a mini-unit within the larger society. Only when the family was no longer successful in meeting individual or family needs did the government step in to provide assistance. Consequently, governmental intervention was perceived by many as undesirable, and the government became the court of last resort where family matters were concerned.

But the historical separation of state and family is not the only source for current conventions surrounding family policy. Because children as a class are political nonentities, adults need to function on their behalf. Traditionally, advocacy groups coalesced to support those who could not advocate for themselves; they addressed conditions of immigrant populations, child labor laws, and so on. Such groups, however, typically were single-focused, advocating a particular response to a particular social problem or need. Hence, competing ideologies and special interests fractured child advocacy efforts (Steiner, 1981). Internal squabbling by those most concerned about children and families prevented the swift passage of legislation. Moynihan, in *Family and Nation* (1986), points out that when Congress attempted to extend Medicare benefits to millions of additional children in 1979, the bill was defeated because of an anti-abortion rider. This fragmentation and adherence to special interests has prevented the formation of a unified children's lobby.

Finally, relationships between the state and the federal government have varied with respect to child and family policy, with the federal government altering its responsibility with each new administration. Such vacillation is problematic because providers are never quite sure of the nature or level of government involvement over the years. Reeling from a heavy federal involvement, the Reagan Administration minimized federal authority while governmental incentives encouraged vast expansion of private sector child care. Brought into existence by changed policies and by throngs of parents who needed services, private-sector programs have expanded dramatically—a case of demographics driving public policy—and private entrepreneurs.

Responding to pressing social conditions has been the modus operandi that characterizes the formation of American child and family policy. Legislative machinery is set in motion when a social problem assumes dimensions of severity for a significant part of society. Steiner says, "When enough families become dysfunctional, public or quasi-public support systems try to take up the slack, that is meet unfulfilled economic, physical or emotional needs" (1981, p. 9). Built on a model that focuses on the deficits or weaknesses of the population to be served, rather than on its strengths and resources, current policies, under attack by liberals and conservatives, only exacerbate family dysfunction. What is AFDC but a family allowance for broken families where one becomes eligible by dissolving, not forming, a family unit (Moynihan, 1986, p. 8)? Murray's *Losing Ground* (1984), an indictment of the welfare system, claims that "social programs and democratic society tend to produce net harm in dealing with the most difficult problems" (p. 218). Dependency has become a more accepted—and more readily available—alternative than employment and self-sufficiency, although the 1988 welfare reform legislation has taken significant steps to redress this ideology.

Alternatives to the residualist/deficit approach that characterize emerging policy are prevalent and may be characterized generally as universalist/holistic strategies. Rooted in a different philosophical orientation, the universal/holistic orientation doesn't target the failings of families; rather it acknowledges that massive social and technological changes (urbanization, industrialization) have brought new conditions which all families need help negotiating. Under this conception, the government should not hand out benefits as solace for failure; instead the government would assure minimum standards of nutrition, health, housing, and education for every citizen as a right. Under such a system, stigmatization associated with receiving government support would ebb as "social welfare becomes accepted as a proper legitimate function of a modern industrial society in helping individuals achieve self-fulfillment" (Wilensky & Lebeaux, 1965, p. 140).

Clearly, the residualist/deficit and universalist/holistic approaches represent extremes in ideology and practice with the residualist/deficit orientation predominating in the area of child and family policy. Recent changes, including those in early education, have been examples of tinkering at the edges of a fundamental policy stance. We have seen that few of the 1980s efforts addressed the major policy questions of equity and fragmentation. In essence, although there appears to be a rash of new policy initiatives in early education, we are at the same fundamental stalemate that characterizes broader policy reform for children and families. A deficit orientation prevails, and where need outdistances what the government has provided, the private sector has surged in to attempt to fill the gap. The consequence is a two-tiered system of service, with differences in ideology, mission, and audience. The nation's preschool children are already stratified with those in need in subsidized programs and those from nondeficit families in nonsubsidized programs. Stated simply, our policy legacy is: (a) a two-tiered approach in early education and (b) an insufficient number of services, particularly for at-risk youngsters.

CRITERIA FOR CHILD AND FAMILY POLICY

There can be no doubt that partisan concerns diminish the opportunity to weld a cohesive and comprehensive child and family policy in the United States. But in spite of disparate views that often call for opposing policy stances, policy makers on both sides of the aisle agree that whatever policy is crafted must be built on the best information available. If knowledge about child and family life were codified into a set of widely accepted principles, principles that were synonymous with quality, then these could be used as a set of criteria against which policies could be evaluated. Free of partisan concerns, principles of development adhere across issues and ideologies. There are general principles, based on years of research, about which there is little disagreement. As such, they can provide useful quality guides for framing basic policy stances. Starting from a basis of objectivity and agreement, nonpartisan principles of child and family development describe what we know to be true rather than that which we believe should be done.

The Principle of Continuity

Children and families benefit if the integrity and continuity of the family can be maintained. The principle of continuity, which is not new, relates to major policy decisions regarding the placement of children in foster care, family dissolution, and custody issues. It also applies to decisions regarding the structure of a young child's day. It is axiomatic that young children benefit from the presence of a loving provider who remains in the child's environment over time. Recently, as early childhood programs are experiencing dramatic staff turnover, continuity has been challenged. Staff come and go so frequently (estimated 41% turnover per year is typical) that children have little time to establish a continuous secure relationship with a caregiver (Clarke-Stewart & Fein, 1983; Phillips & Howes, 1987).

Policy decisions and program plans that promote frequent mobility of young children from one provider to the next, or from one setting to another, should be minimized. The principle of continuity demands that when early education policies are being developed, attention be paid to minimizing fragmentation and to creating a system where continuity is maximized.

The Principle of Heterogeneity

Children and families have their own individual natures and vary on every measurable characteristic. Because of this heterogeneity, children and families have diverse needs. The policy implications of this principle are that families need options and that those options must meet the needs of the involved individuals. Scholars (Gamble & Zigler, 1986) have emphasized that instead of considering general program outcomes, we must go further to ask how different *types* of programs affect different *types* of children. In the same way, the needs and resources of individual families must be considered when formulating policy and mounting programs. For instance, a single model of early education—say a half-day program—will not meet the needs of all parents who want preschool services. To meet the needs of working and nonworking families, services for young children must vary within communities. Further, within these services, the individual needs of children must be met with developmentally appropriate activities and options.

To facilitate the establishment of rich options within a community, there must be some method of cooperative planning across funding agencies. Programs must be sited to optimize community need, and flexibility in programming must be encouraged.

Minimum Environmental Level

Children and families who experience an environment that falls below a minimum threshold of quality will be damaged by that environment. Typically, when we speak of environment, a physical setting is implied. This principle uses the word environment to include both physical and social milieus, and concerns such diverse elements as nutrition, safety, medical care (including prenatal care for pregnant women), and a stimulating social and intellectual environment.

For young children, the quality of environment is critical at home and in preschool settings. Issues regarding regulation have been widely debated for decades, and yet the nation still has no federal regulations for child care. Each state has its own licensing standard. Most states, in fact, have two standards, one for included facilities, and one for exempt settings. The degree to which these standards vary, and to which variation is acceptable, are policy questions that confront early childhood professionals. Though addressed, the issues surrounding standards have not been resolved in the late 1980s reforms.

Debate over child care standards not only concerns the physical milieu that surrounds young children when they are in preschool programs, but also focuses on what should constitute the child's socioeducational environment. What are the appropriate requisites for the training of those who work with young children? What should be the content of the curriculum? How great an emphasis on academics is appropriate? What happens to children when they are pushed too far too soon? In the current wave of 1980s initiatives, these questions are being widely addressed. While there is no consensus yet, recent research on various curriculum models (Schweinhart, Weikart, & Larner, 1986) cautions against rapid endorsement of highly academic and structured approaches.

Parents have traditionally acted on behalf of their children in making decisions which have historically been assumed to be correct, unbiased by self-interest or insufficient knowledge. The needs of the parent, however, may not always be congruent with those of the child. This poses particular dilemmas when parents are forced to select child care or preschool programs from among choices that are poor in quality or insufficient in scope. The parent who needs a full-day program that parallels the working day may have a child who needs greater continuity of care or a better environment than the available—and affordable—full-day programs can provide. On the other hand, the available high-quality programs may be too costly for parents, or may not run all day. These are only examples of incongruity between child and parent needs. Although policymakers must heed developmental principles in formulating policies and designing programs, it is crucial that the programs consider the needs of both child and parent.

The Child and Family Context

Although the family is the most important influence on the child, numerous other institutions affect the child's development—schools, religious settings, the media, and child care. The implication of this principle is that the child is affected, both directly and indirectly, by community and societal events. A plant closing or corporate personnel policies may influence the child as profoundly as policies that appear more germane. It is thus imperative for policymakers to realize that when they are voting on social policies that do not appear to be directly related to youngsters, they may in reality be affecting children's lives in critical ways.

Taken together, these principles provide a general framework against which policy initiatives for young children can be reviewed and measured. They do not commend particular policy stances, but may forestall the development of policies detrimental to young children. Given the plethora of policy initiatives being launched by the states and given the consensus on these principles, are there specific policy recommendations that should be followed as we move into the next decade?

THE GOVERNMENT'S ROLE IN EARLY CARE AND EDUCATION: THE NEXT DECADE

The nature of early childhood education is such that its services must remain under local and state auspices, with local providers and parents having the right and responsibility to tailor their programs to the needs of the community and the needs of the participating children and families. Further, any plan that affects the lives of young children should adhere to developmental principles that acknowledge the child's need for continuity, the uniqueness of the individual, the primacy of the parent, and the need for comprehensive services.

With primary responsibility for program implementation lodged at the local level, what are the appropriate roles for the state and for the federal government in the field of early childhood education? States are in a unique position because they license staff and programs, set standards, establish monitoring procedures, and can enjoin parties to cooperate in joint program planning. In addition, states are in a unique position to examine alternative funding strategies and delivery systems, and select the most appropriate. For states in which no state-based comprehensive early childhood program presently exists, this prospect is particularly exciting.

The range of options for states' participation in early care and education is wide. They can expand existing delivery systems, through education, human services, or Head Start. This tack, dominant in the current wave of early childhood efforts, has liabilities in that it does little to avoid problems of equity, fragmentation, and standardization. It does not advance the field, although it does increase the number of slots open for youngsters. An alternative though by no means complete approach, refundable tax credits could provide benefits to some of the population. However, increasing tax credits does little to address the longstanding problems facing the field. States may also consider directing school aid formula funds to include preschool efforts. This strategy has the liability of favoring school-based programs, and in some states wealthier districts, also without redressing the fundamental issues of the field.

If a state is serious about rectifying the fragmentation, uneven quality, and lack of equity in the field, in addition to providing more direct services, it could consider establishing a special office that cuts across agency lines. This office would be responsible for coordinating early care and education efforts in the state. In order to be successful, the office needs sufficient authority and a clear understanding of its facilitative mission. Establishing an interagency office within an existing agency is a variation that may work if the office has sufficient staff and influence.

Because of the states' ubiquitous authority in teacher licensing and certification, the state can use its leverage to insist on quality in early childhood programs. From the National Day Care Study (Ruopp, Travers, Glantz, & Coelen, 1979), we know that teacher training and experience in early childhood is critical to a program's success. At a minimum, states must ensure that all teachers in early childhood programs have requisite training and experience. Precautions must be taken to ensure that elementary certification is not equated with early childhood competency. Beyond this essential step, states should pursue innovative approaches to credentialing and take leadership in developing career ladders that recognize the competencies of experienced providers. States should also ensure that quality early childhood training and placement opportunities are afforded teachers in training. The primary criterion for field placements for teachers in training should be program quality, not program auspices.

States need to resist the temptation to respond to providers of care who call for reduced standards for staff or for centers (Child Care Review, 1987). The suggestion that more stringent standards deplete the supply of available care and force children into unlicensed environments is both a short-sighted and an ill-founded rationale.

Finally, when states expand their services to young children, they must not skirt issues of equity, of fragmentation between public and private programs, or of diversity between care and education. States need to address these issues and to allocate funding in a manner that ensures not simply expanded service, but also improved delivery of those services. States must acknowledge that their responsibility is not merely providing additional slots for children, but that they have a leadership role in seeking fundamental solutions to the problems confronting the profession. Ultimately, such an investment will reduce duplication and prevent the proliferation of low-quality programs.

Clearly, this vision places primary responsibility at the local and state levels, but it does not obviate a role for the federal government in early childhood. Ideally, the federal government would assume a leadership function, identifying and providing the means to address some of the above mentioned critical elements. This should be handled by establishing a research capacity so that knowledge garnered regarding program implementation and effects could be assessed systematically and applied to the construction of new policies. The federal government should take responsibility for chronicling existing innovative efforts and, through a process like the National Diffusion Network in education, disseminate information on effective programs in schools, Head Start, day care, after-school, and family day care. In addition, such a resource should chronicle innovative funding strategies at the state level and creative efforts that seek to reduce fragmentation and inequity in the field. By making knowledge of these efforts available throughout the nation, early childhood could build upon itself, rather than reinventing the wheel in each state or municipality.

To assist the early childhood field, the federal government should consider funding demonstration projects that ameliorate problems endemic to the field. Such programs should encourage collaboration between the public and private sector; address the problem of attracting and retaining high-quality individuals into a field characterized by low salaries and low morale; minimize existing inequities for children and adults, by establishing pensions or equitable salaries for early childhood workers; and assess the viability of establishing guidelines for programs. Further, the federal government should establish the capability and willingness to help the field deal with unexpected occurrences. For example, the child care insurance crisis that forced so many centers out of business should have been accorded priority status and supports should have been made available to programs in need.

To accomplish these goals, a federal office of early childhood education should be established. Such an office should have responsibility for federal efforts on behalf of preschool youngsters. The office should bridge the gap between all offices that deal with early childhood issues in, for example, the Department of Education, the Department of Health, and the Administration for Children, Youth and Families. Such leadership is the least that a caring society can provide for its youngest citizens.

In conclusion, in a field as complex as early education, in a time as complex as the 1980s, it was a miracle that so much has been accomplished on behalf of young children and their families. However, while we may take pride in these accomplishments, we must be less complacent and more self-critical.

Recent accomplishments in the field of early childhood must be supplemented by the efforts of individuals who are willing to tackle the hard issues and make the difficult choices. It is the responsibility of quality institutions and far-sighted individuals to set a standard that does not accept "more of the same" as better. If the profession of early childhood is to advance, it must not set its sights solely on increasing the numbers of children receiving services in the field, but on changing those things that, to date, have remained the same, to address the recalcitrant issues which threaten to quash the exuberance and vitality that has long characterized early care and education programs.

REFERENCES

Bane, M.J. (1978). *Family policy in the United States: Toward a description and evaluation* (Working Paper No. 52). Cambridge, MA: Joint Center for Urban Studies of the Massachusetts Institute of Technology and Harvard University.

Barbaro, F. (1979, November). The case against family policy. *Social Work, 24*(6), 455-457.

Berrueta-Clement, J.R., Schweinhart, L.J., Barnett, W.S., Epstein, A.S., & Weikart, D.F. (1984). *Changed lives: The effects of the Perry Preschool Program on youths through age nineteen.* Ypsilanti, MI: High/Scope Press.

Blank, H., & Wilkins, A. (1985). *Child care: Whose priority? A state child care fact book.* Washington, DC: Children's Defense Fund.

Bronfenbrenner, U. (1979). *The ecology of human development: Experiments by nature and design.* Cambridge, MA: Harvard University Press.

Brown v. Board of Education. (1954). 347 U.S. 483.

Child Care Review. (1987, April). Are state standards too high for child care? *Child Care Review, 2*(5), 6-12.

Children's Defense Fund. (1988). *A call for action to make our nation safe for children: A briefing book on the status of American children in 1988.* Washington, DC: Author.

Clarke-Stewart, K.A., & Fein, G. (1983). Early childhood programs. In *Handbook of Child Psychology: Volume 2, Infancy and Developmental Psychology.* New York: John Wiley & Sons.

Cohen, S.B. (1986, March). *Take a giant step: An equal start in education for all New York City four-year-olds.* Final report of the Early Childhood Education Commission, New York.

Committee for Economic Development. (1987). *Children in need: Investment strategies for the educationally disadvantaged.* Washington, DC: Author.

Council of Chief State School Officers. (1988, September 6). *Guide for Chief's initiative: State action on early childhood and parent education, and related services.* Draft paper for CCSSO Study Commission Review, Washington, DC.

Crain, R.L., & Mahard, R.E. (1978, Summer). Desegregation and black achievement: A review of reserach. *Law and Contemporary Problems, 42.*

Dempsey, J.J. (1981). *The family and public policy: The issue of the 1980s.* Baltimore, MD: Paul H. Brookes Publishers.

Feldman, H. (1979, August). Why we need a family policy. *Journal of Marriage and the Family, 41*(3), 453-455.

Friedman, D.C. (1988, April 1). *Memo "Employer Supported Child Care."* New York: The Conference Board.

Gamble, T.J., & Zigler, E. (1986). Effects of infant day care: Another look at the evidence. *American Journal of Orthopsychiatry, 56,* 26-42.

Grubb, W.N. (1986). *Young children face the states: Issues and options for early childhood programs.* Unpublished manuscript, Rutgers University, Center for Policy Research in Education, New Brunswick, NJ.

Hawley, W.D. (Ed.). (1981). *Effective school desegregation: Equity, quality and feasibility.* Beverly Hills, CA: Sage.

Johnson, A.S., III, et al. (1978). *Toward an inventory of federal programs with direct impact on families.* Washington, DC: Institute for Educational Leadership, George Washington University.

Kagan, S.L. (Ed.). (1985). *Four year olds: Who is responsible?* Hartford, CT: Connecticut State Department of Education.

Kagan, S.L., Klugman, E., & Zigler, E.F. (1983). Shaping child and family policies: Criteria and strategies for a new decade. In E.F. Zigler, S.L. Kagan, & E. Klugman (Eds.), *Children, families and government: Perspectives on American social policy.* New York: Cambridge University Press.

Kahn, A.J., & Kamerman, S.B. (1987). *Child care: Facing the hard choices.* Dover, MA: Auburn House.

Kamerman, S.B., & Kahn, A.J. (1978). *Family policy: Government and families in fourteen countries.* New York: Columbia University Press.

Lazar, I., & Darlington, R. (1982). Lasting effects of early education: A report from the Consortium for Longitudinal Studies. *Monographs of the Society for Research in Child Development, 47*(2-3, Serial No. 195).

Marmor, T.R. (1983). Competing perspectives on social policy. In E.F. Zigler, S.L. Kagan, & E. Klugman (Eds.), *Children, families and government: Perspectives on American social policy.* New York: Cambridge University Press.

Marx, F., & Seligson, M. (1988). *The public school early childhood study: The state survey.* New York: Bank Street College of Education.

Moroney, R.M. (1979, August). The issue of family policy: Do we know enough to take action? *Journal of Marriage and the Family, 41*(3), 461-463.

Moynihan, D.P. (1965, September 18). A family policy for the nation. *America,* pp. 280-283.

Moynihan, D.P. (1986). *Family and nation.* New York: Harcourt Brace Jovanovich.

Murray, C. (1984). *Losing ground.* New York: Basic Books.

National Governors' Association & Center for Policy Research. (1987, July). *The first sixty months: A handbook for promising preventing programs for children 0-5 years of age.* Washington, DC: National Governors' Association.

Phillips, D.A., & Howes, C. (1987). Indicators of quality in child care: Review of research, In D. A. Phillips (Ed.), *Quarterly in child care: What does research tell us?* Washington, DC: National Association for the Education of Young Children.

Ruopp, R., Travers, J., Glantz, F., & Coelen, C. (1979). *Children at the center: Final report of the National Day Care Study: Summary findings and their implications.* Cambridge, MA: Abt Books.

Schweinhart, L. (1985). *Early childhood development programs in the eighties: The national picture,* Ypsilanti, MI: High/Scope Early Childhood Policy Papers.

Schweinhart, L., Weikart, D.P., & Larner, M.B. (1986). Consequences of three preschool curriculum models through age 15. *Early Childhood Research Quarterly, 1*(1), 15-45.

Steiner, G.Y. (1981). *The futility of family policy.* Washington, DC: Brookings Institution.

U.S. Department of Education. (1986). *Pre-school enrollment: Trends and implications.* Washington, DC: U.S. Government Printing Office (065-000-00276-1).

U.S. Department of Labor. (1977). *Dictionary of occupational titles, fourth edition.* Washington, DC: U.S. Government Printing Office.

Weil, J. (1986). *One third more: Maine Head Start expansion with state funds.* Ellsworth, ME: Federal-State Partnership Project, Action Opportunities.

Weinberg, M. (1975). The relationship between school desegregation and academic achievement: A review of the research. *Law and Contemporary Problems, 39*, 240-270.

Wilensky, H.L., & Lebeaux, C.N. (1965). *Industrial society and social welfare.* New York: The Free Press.

Zigler, E.F. (1979). Head Start: Not a program but an evolving concept. In E. Zigler & J. Valentine (Eds.), *Project Head Start: A legacy of the war on poverty.* New York: The Free Press.

Zigler, E.F. (1986, May). Should four-year-olds be in school? *Principal, 65*(5), 10-14.

3
Private Foundations: What Is Their Role In Improving The Education of Disadvantaged Youth?

M. Hayes Mizell

Several weeks ago, I was talking with a businessman who is the chairman of a statewide Governor's Policy Council on At Risk Youth. He expressed his frustration with trying to get members of the Council, all of whom chair the boards of major state agencies, to recognize that schools must change if they are going to educate at-risk young people more effectively. The members of the Council wanted to urge local school systems to adopt a well-known program that is being used in many of the nation's urban areas. The Council chairman, however, was skeptical about this proposal, because in his view the program served only a few at risk youth. It did not seem to have the potential to change schools. He tried to get his colleagues on the Council to understand the need for recommendations that would cause schools to alter fundamentally the ways they serve disadvantaged students. "What is that expression?," he asked. "'If it ain't broke, don't fix it'? Well, it *is* broke, and we've *got* to fix it!"

This is more than just the exasperation of one frustrated business-man. From every quarter of our society we are hearing that the public schools are failing to educate effectively not only disadvantaged students, but average students as well. The April 16, 1989 edition of *The New York Times* represents the pervasive nature of this indictment. In Section 9 of the paper, there was an article entitled, "Experts Divided on Jobs in the 90's." The article consisted of a dialogue among a half-dozen authors, researchers, and policy analysts, and covered a variety range of subjects. Predictably, one of the experts stated, "The number of people who have high school diplomas and college degrees who cannot communicate is amazing. They can't write, spell, or speak clearly; and we're not talking about dropouts."

Another panelist shared the observation, "I am seeing business suddenly worried about illiteracy, or minimal literacy skills and minimal logical abilities in the incoming work force. They never worried about it before." Still another expert said, "I find, with more and more government and business people I talk to in many different countries, that the business of societies is learning. The global positioning of countries more and more is going to be the extent to which they have a problem-solving population."

The same issue of the *Times*, in Section 4, included the weekly column of Albert Shanker, the President of the American Federation of Teachers. Shanker devoted his column to sharing findings from a February 1989 report of the National Assessment of Education Progress (NAEP). The NAEP report, *Crossroads in American Education*, presented an overview of the organization's 20 years of student assessment in reading, writing, and science. At the conclusion of his column, Shanker summarized the NAEP report with the statement, "About half of our in-school 17-year-olds could not do math much beyond adding, subtracting and multiplying with whole numbers, and few could provide enough information in their writing exercises to communicate their ideas. In other words, most of them don't qualify for good jobs." And finally, in the first section of the April 16th *Times*, there was an article that described the context in which many urban school children receive an inadequate education. The article, "Tug-of-War for Black Youth's Hearts," described a mentoring program in Washington, DC, and its efforts to exert a positive influence on black children who live in dangerous neighborhoods. One of the children in the mentoring program is a 9-year-old. He lives in a housing project with his four siblings and his 25-year-old mother who dropped out of school after ninth grade. "Drugs and violence is all over here," said the mother. "It's in the houses, on the streets. I worry about my kids all the time." Her goal for her son is to "finish high school and maybe go to college."

These reports from one day's *New York Times* illustrate the twin dilemmas of public education in America. First, because of the changing nature of our national economy and the labor needs of business and industry, our schools are not doing a good job of preparing most young people to become productive and self-sufficient.

Second, there are large numbers of disadvantaged youth for whom even this inadequate education remains an elusive goal.

The response to these problems has come primarily from state legislatures. After all, states are primarily responsible for public policy education in this nation, and it is appropriate that much of the leadership for education reform should come from this quarter. Ironically, states which have had the longest and most devastating experience with the neglect of public education—Arkansas, South Carolina, Tennessee, and Florida—have also been leaders in the education reform movement (Education Commission of the States, 1988). Perhaps more than other states, they understand the consequences of failing to invest in the future. Regardless of their motivation, states are now appropriating more money for public schools, and engaging in numerous reforms, ranging from encouraging more students to participate in advanced programs, to requiring more math and science units for graduation, to experimenting with school-based decision making.

A handful of school systems also seem to be moving beyond incremental improvements to initiating a major overhaul of the schools. Pittsburgh, Miami, San Diego, Memphis, and Cincinnati are among the school systems that policy analysts cite as leaders in the process of local education reform (Hill, Wise, & Shapiro, 1989).

In spite of the energetic efforts of some states and local school systems, education reform is proceeding at a painfully slow pace. In most schools, little has changed. Teachers still talk *to* students rather than work *with* them, expectations continue to be low for disadvantaged students, and schools seldom challenge, provoke, engage, or stimulate young people. Schools still pay too much attention to the students who learn independently, and they pay too little attention to those who suffer from academic and personal neglect. Worst of all, most schools do not balance the mastery of basic skills with the process of learning how to learn, and the attainment of understanding. According to Rexford Brown (1988), director of the Higher Literacies Project at the Education Commission of the States, "Schooling places heavy emphasis on drill, memorization, recitation, seatwork, and teacher talk...almost no intensive reading takes place, no extensive writing, and no classroom discussion or debate."

The important task for those seeking to reform public education is not to define the schools' problems or to pose countless and often conflicting remedies. Rather, the challenge is to bring about changes in behaviors and practices so that students become more knowledgeable and creative.

State legislatures have tried to change practices at the building level. They have created accountability and testing programs which encourage teachers to focus their instruction so it will produce measurable results. Because of state mandates, teachers may, for example, emphasize math skills, and within the context of a statewide testing program, more students may be able to demonstrate their mastery of these skills. While policymakers may have enabled students to improve their performance on standardized tests, they cannot assume that students have a better *understanding* of mathematics, nor that they will be able to *apply* the skills they have allegedly learned. Legislatures, therefore, may have succeeded in changing teachers' behaviors, but it does not necessarily mean that they have achieved the education reform that will prepare students for life in the next century.

Another potential advocate for building-level change, the federal government, has almost withdrawn from the field of education reform. The United States Congress has continued to support and improve compensatory education, vocational education, and programs for students with handicapping conditions, but the executive branch has restricted its role to fact finding, rhetoric from the bully pulpit, and recognition programs. Except for the catalytic effect of the Department of Education's release of *A Nation At Risk*, the executive branch has yet to show that it has an effective strategy for achieving education reform at the local level.

It is also unlikely that the recent education proposals of the Bush Administration will cause administrators and teachers to change their current practices. The proposed "Presidential Merit Schools" program would provide cash rewards to schools that make substantial progress in raising students' educational performance. If enacted, this program will tell us what we already know, that it is possible to improve schools dramatically. "Improving" schools will be rewarded, but few if any schools undertake major reforms simply to qualify for the rewards. The program will neither encourage nor require plans to raise academic achievement ("Bush proposes," 1989).

The proposed "Magnet Schools of Excellence" program would support the establishment, expansion, or enhancement of magnet schools. According to a U.S. Department of Education official, these magnet schools would "offer high-quality instruction...through curricula and activities of an exceptional or innovative nature." While any effort to encourage high-quality education is helpful, experience has demonstrated that magnet schools do not usually produce better education for the economically and educationally disadvantaged children who remain in regular schools.

Like state legislatures and the federal government, some private foundations would also like to encourage education reform. However, foundations have no power or control over local schools, and their resources are minute when compared to the amounts of local, state, or federal appropriations for public elementary and secondary education.

It is impossible to generalize about grant-making foundations, because the only traits they share are that they must adhere to federal law, they have boards of trustees, and they provide financial support. In all other ways they differ—in the size of their assets, the amount of money they distribute, how they consider proposals and make grants, and what they expect to achieve from their grant making.

Even though there are 27,000 active grant-making foundations in the United States, with total assets of $115 billion, these numbers are deceptive. Of the 27,000 foundations, only 6,410 account for 96 percent of the assets and 87 percent of the grant dollars. A further examination of these 6,410 foundations reveals that only 150 of them account for 55 percent of all foundation assets, and they award 38 percent of all foundation grant dollars, most of these funds went to colleges and universities. Elementary and secondary schools received a total of only $61 million, and this includes nonpublic schools (Renz, 1989).

For most people, the word "foundation" evokes images of money sought and given with little effort. Most people who have worked to either obtain grants or make them would disagree with this perception. Before an organization receives a grant it has usually invested a great deal of time, money, and labor in searching for a foundation that may be responsive to its mission and needs. After a grant seeker has identified such a foundation, the organization's staff has to make themselves known to the foundation. Over a period of many months, they must develop a relationship with foundation staff, and establish credibility. In the end, foundations turn down many more grant proposals than they fund.

Even the process of *grant making* is not as easy as it may appear. Federal law requires each foundation to pay out annually in grants and contributions amounts equal to 4.25 percent of the foundation's net assets. This means, for example, that each year a foundation with one million dollars in assets must make grants or contributions totaling at least $42,500. Foundations with $100 million dollars in assets must annually pay out at least $4.25 million each year. Some foundations pay out the minimum required, and others go beyond the minimum.

Foundations respond differently to the federal requirement to disburse a certain percentage of their assets each year. A small foundation without staff, or with part-time staff, may make grants based on a limited awareness of needs, because the foundation only has the capacity to respond to needs identified by trustees, or by determined grant seekers. If a philanthropist narrowly defines a foundation's purpose, such as providing scholarships for impoverished students from eastern Kentucky to attend the University of Cincinnati, the foundation may not find it necessary to have a grant-making strategy because the purpose of the foundation is very specific. On the other hand, a foundation with a broad mission, relatively large assets, active trustees, and adequate staff has more opportunities to take initiative in defining needs and considering how to best respond to them. Creative grant making, however, is more a function of the trustees' and staff's level of energy and insight than it is the size of the foundation's assets.

The $61 million which foundations contributed to elementary and secondary schools in 1987 is less than the annual budget of one public school system with an enrollment of 20,000 students. Considering that this $61 million includes grants to independent schools, the amount made available to public education is even smaller. Foundations are not only reluctant to support publicly financed institutions, but they question whether public schools are making the best use of the resources currently available to them. And in light of the large budgets of most public school systems, foundations wonder whether their relatively modest support can make a real difference. Will the activity which the foundation is supporting produce significant change in the school system, or will it be overwhelmed by the system's bureaucratic, political, and financial infrastructure? These are legitimate concerns, validated by difficult lessons foundations have learned in supporting urban school reform.

There is, perhaps, one strategy that presents an opportunity for foundations seeking a way to encourage and support education reform that will enable schools to more effectively serve disadvantaged youth. The current emphasis on what education reformers call "school-based governance," "school site management," or "school-based decision making" may provide an opening. Whatever term we use to describe it, school-based governance means that administrators, teachers, and citizens at the building level assume greater responsibility for improving their school.

There is potential for school-based decision making to produce genuine reform and increase the academic achievement of disadvantaged youth. We know that schools serving large numbers of disadvantaged youth are not as effective as they should be. Dramatic change is required. We also know there are limits to the effectiveness of changes mandated by the federal government, by state legislatures, or even by local school boards. In the end, the education of disadvantaged students depends on administrators and teachers at the building level. If they cannot fashion, or as Phil Schlechty says, "invent" a school to raise these students' achievement levels, it is not likely to get done.

Administrators and teachers do not have all the answers, but they do not need them. They can draw upon abundant informational resources, based on experience and research, that describe how to better educate disadvantaged youth. We already know that disadvantaged young people can perform at high levels, and that the actions of administrators and teachers can help them do so. The first step is for a leader or a leadership group at the school level to *believe* that disadvantaged youth can master high content. The second step is to *decide* that the school must undergo major changes to enable disadvantaged young people to achieve at higher levels. Through school-based decision making, administrators, teachers, and citizens can make the decisions, and monitor and evaluate the implementation necessary to reform the education of disadvantaged youth.

The task of education reform is demanding. The federal government, state legislatures, and local superintendents have found it difficult to make education reform take hold. It will not be easier just because it is the responsibility of people at the school site. In some ways, education reform will be more difficult under school-based decision making. Unlike reforms foisted onto the schools by legislatures or school boards, improvements resulting from school-based decision making will have to be carried out by those initiating the reforms. This may be an advantage because the reforms may be more realistic.

It can also be a disadvantage because the decision-making team may compromise their own "reforms." The teams may make assumptions about what is and is not "possible" based on their sensitivity to the culture and the relationships in the school. A state legislature cannot know that the opposition of one sixth-grade teacher in one school can sabotage the implementation of education reform legislation, but that school's decision-making team will know. The success of education reform at the building level may depend on whether the team will use its knowledge to win over or circumvent that teacher, or whether the team concludes that reform is secondary to maintaining good personal relationships.

Education reform through school-based decision making may also collapse under the enormity of the task. Michael Cohen (1988) points out that "the primary issues to be resolved at the school site level have to do with identifying structural and organizational features of schools that need to be altered to...[help] all students acquire higher order skills...enhance [their] sense of self-worth and competence...[and] provide an environment in which students receive personal attention." Cohen goes on to say, "a starting point" for change "are those conditions of instruction known to be related to student learning.

These include educational goals, the structure of knowledge, instructional tasks and activities, instructional group size and composition, and instructional time (pp. 8–9).

It is hard to imagine administrators, teachers, and citizens at the building level taking on these issues. School boards and superintendents in most urban areas do not expect this type of school-based decision making, they do not provide the opportunity for it to occur, and they do not support it. Even where system-level school officials embrace school-based decision making, they frequently emphasize a governance process which in reality means more autonomy for the principal but limited participation for teachers and citizens. In other places, school-based decision making is characterized by increased teacher involvement, but not necessarily for the purpose of altering "the conditions of education known to be related to student learning." There is also evidence that state and local public officials are much more inclined to advocate school-based decision making than they are to yield the power necessary for it to work.[1]

In spite of these drawbacks, it is likely that only school-based decision making teams, composed of administrators, teachers, and citizens can plan and implement lasting education reform. This process will not occur by itself. Advocates for education reform must encourage and support it.

As a result of a recent grants competition, the Edna McConnell Clark Foundation has witnessed the potential of school-based decision making. The competition involved school systems interested in providing a more substantive and challenging education to disadvantaged youth in the middle grades. To begin the competitive process, the Foundation invited 20 urban school systems to send teams to a conference organized by the National Foundation for the Improvement

---

[1] In an effort to institute school-based improvements, New York State and the [New York City] central Board of Education created the Comprehensive School Improvement Project (CSIP) in 1985. Committees, composed of parents, teachers, and administrators, were formed at "low achieving" schools for the purpose of developing strategies to improve each particular school. Independent evaluations, however, have revealed that the project is little more than a paper exercise at many schools. Schools are evaluated on the results of standardized test scores. There is little scrutiny of whether schools ever implement CSIP plans as long as these scores, which are easy to manipulate, go up. Even where CSIP is taken seriously, schools have neither the power nor the resources to make real changes ("A blueprint," 1989). On the other hand, Chicago School Reform Act, each Chicago school will be governed by a Local School Council consisting of the principal, six parents elected by parents, two community residents elected by community residents, and two teachers elected by the school's staff. One of the powers of the council is to "directly appoint, upon seven affirmative votes, a new principal to serve under a three-year performance contract." The legislation takes effect beginning with the 1989-1990 school year.

of Education (NFIE, 1988). Each team was composed of no more than 10 people, including at least two principals, two teachers from each of the schools represented by the principals, a representative of the superintendent, and a community leader.

The conference was led by three outside consultants with expertise in adolescent development and education. Each of them made presentations of approximately an hour-and-a-half. Afterwards, the team spent two-and-a-half days reflecting on and assessing the implications of the information provided by the consultants, and planning for widespread change in their schools.

At the conclusion of the conference, the benefits of this process became apparent. Teachers reported that they are rarely involved in seminal discussions about school change or have an opportunity to reexamine their assumptions about what reforms are possible. They said they almost never get to work as peers with school district officials or even their principals on issues of school improvement. Because of the spirit of camaraderie, and the time to develop as a group, the teams left the conference enthusiastic about the potential to better educate disadvantaged youth.

As the next step in the grants competition, the Foundation invited 12 of the school systems to develop proposals for possible major funding. School systems were asked to design their proposals around four objectives disadvantaged students should be able to achieve by the time they enter the 10th grade.[2] It was the responsibility of the school systems to set forth in their proposals how they would achieve these objectives. Each school system school was provided with a $10,000 planning grant, access to technical assistance, and five months to develop a proposal.

In the request for proposal, the Foundation asked each school system to assemble a proposal development team (Mizell & Fleming, 1988). The RFP suggested, but did not require, that a majority of the team be composed of people who would be directly responsible for implementing the proposal. Most school systems formed their team by adding to the group that had attended the NFIE conference.

The RFP asked each school system and at least two of its schools to describe how the school system and the schools would "develop and

---

[2] The objectives were stated as follows: "Between the time disadvantaged youth leave grade five and enter grade ten, they will: (1) Remain in school and complete the middle grades curriculum, on time; (2) Exhibit mastery of higher order reasoning, thinking, and comprehension skills; (3) Exhibit improved self-esteem, self-efficacy, and attitudes toward school and schoolwork, as a result of regularly engaging in supportive interactions with adults; (4) Enter high school with an understanding of how different curriculums can affect their career and/or postsecondary education options (Edna McConnell Clark Foundation, 1988).

provide an education of high expectations, high content, and high support" for disadvantaged youth in the middle grades. Each of the schools were also required to have a proposal development team, with at least some of the members also serving on the school system team.

At the conclusion of the proposal development process, the team members were enthusiastic about their experience. Team members felt they had participated in a critical activity—developing a plan for transforming their schools. Teachers said they had been energized and renewed by having the responsibility to examine their schools from a problem-solving perspective. They felt their opinions were both valued. In addition, they had the opportunity to learn new information and to consider its relevance to their schools.

The teams were so enthusiastic about the plans *they* developed they said they would use their proposals as a blueprint for change, even if they did not receive funding. Some teams even acknowledged that while they hoped to receive a grant, they realized the schools' major problems required more changes in attitudes than money.

This experience suggests several potential roles for private, community, and corporate foundations. Through their grant making, foundations can communicate to public school systems in urban areas that they recognize the importance of school-based decision making as a tool for education reform. School systems, like private organizations, are eager to receive not only the money, but the recognition that is implicit in a foundation grant. Because the process of obtaining a grant is competitive, the public perceives the recipient of a foundation grant as a "winner" or as "worthy." This is how school systems would like to be seen by the public. A grant advances a school system's public relations as well as its financial and programmatic interests. For these reasons, school systems can be receptive to how foundations frame their guidelines for grant making. A school system may have an interest in school-based decision making as a concept, but it may lack the incentive to initiate such a process. However, if a foundation announces that it is interested in supporting school-based decision making, the school system may rise to the opportunity and consider this means of achieving education reform. Foundations can, therefore, play a valuable role in causing school systems to consider school-based decision making as an important issue.

One of the problems with decision making at the building level is that educators may see it as an objective of reform, rather than as an activity intended to bring about quality education. Just because administrators, teachers, and citizens make decisions at the school site does not necessarily mean that the students' education will improve. If schools focus on school-based decision making as anything other than a means to achieve improved student performance, they will have misused this tool of education reform. Foundations can help assure that school-based decisionmaking is more likely to benefit students, rather than decision makers, by supporting programs that use this process to achieve a specific instructional purpose. The decision-making task may be as fundamental as developing what Mike Cohen calls "a map, or a vision, of what [a] restructured [school] might look like." This is an obvious starting point for many school-based decision-making teams. It is not appropriate for a foundation to tell a school system what to do, but foundations can provide a challenge which school systems can choose to pursue, or not.

Aside from encouraging school-based decision making itself, and providing some focus for this process, foundation dollars can provide support which is essential if school-based decision making is to work. If a team of administrators, teachers, and citizens are going to provide leadership to restructure their school, they need the time to meet, to study, and to plan. But educators at the building level are very much involved in what Ted Sizer calls the "extraordinary dailiness of keeping a good school." They are not only engaged in the day-to-day task of delivering educational services, but they must respond to a wide range of demands on their time, from unanticipated crises to bureaucratic routines necessary to satisfy the central office and the state department of education. There is simply little time left for the study and reflection that any good decision-making process requires.

Educators at the building level are also very isolated. They usually have little voice in planning for staff development, and the in-service education provided by the central office seems to have little to do with either meeting the educators' needs, or preparing them to implement education reforms. Teachers do not routinely read such major education periodicals as *Education Week, Educational Leadership,* or *Phi Delta Kappan,* and they seldom have the opportunity to attend well-planned, germane, and challenging education conferences. Teachers may know what is going on in their school, but too many of them do not know what is going on in a comparable school down the street, or across town. The result of this isolation is what one teacher has called "the mental lethargy the school system encourages." One of the benefits of school-based decision making is that it can empower educators to take more responsibility for their own continuing education. Reformers' concerns about developing "lifelong learners" are as applicable to building-level educators as to students.

By supporting school-based decision making, foundations can help these break out of the "mental lethargy" and isolation that make it so difficult for schools to reform themselves. A school system can use a foundation grant to hire substitute teachers and provide release time for regular classroom teachers to participate on a decision-making team. Foundation support can provide subscriptions to major education periodicals for all team members, and help send the entire team, including community representatives, to conferences and workshops that relate to the team's task. The team may also benefit from involving outside experts at the school site. As the team begins its work, an outside, independent facilitator may be useful to keep the team on task and to help ensure that no one person or group of persons dominate the team's deliberations. The team may also wish to have direct access to consultants who can provide expertise on the issue that the team is addressing. With foundation support, decision-making teams can get the help needed to identify and review alternative practices, and to plan and implement changes necessary to better educate disadvantaged youth.

This is not to suggest that support for school-based decision making is the only appropriate role for foundations to play in encouraging school reform. Grants to research, advocacy, and school support organizations are essential. However, the potential of school-based decision making does suggest there may be greater payoffs from support for this activity than foundations have realized. Particularly for corporate and community foundation, and even for public education funds, it may be time to reassess the effect of initiatives that support teacher workshops, minigrants for teachers, the purchase of computers and software, and tutoring and mentoring programs. These activities can have a positive impact, but they can have a greater impact when they are an integral part of a school's *carefully developed design* for major change.

Foundations, like the federal government and the states, can support but cannot achieve school reform. That is the task of administrators, teachers, and citizens at the building level. They must decide whether their schools are willing to challenge, engage, and support disadvantaged students in achieving higher levels. School-based decision making can help a building-level leadership team reach that decision, and execute it. As policy analysts at the RAND Corporation have pointed out, education reform "means using policy less to mandate resource allocation, structures, and rules, and more to initiate development. It means commissioning people who work in real schools to fashion workable solutions to real problems, and allowing those solutions the opportunity to fail and the time to succeed (Elmore & McCoughlin, 1988, p. 61)." For this to occur, school boards and superintendents must expect greater leadership from the building level, they must permit it to occur, and they must provide opportunities for that leadership to be nurtured.

REFERENCES

Brown, R. (1988, Spring). Schooling and thoughtfulness. *Basic education: Issues, answers & facts* (Vol. 3, No. 3). Washington, DC: Council for Basic Education.

Bush proposes FY 1990 $422 million initiative, adds $31 million to voc ed. (1989, April 12). *Employment and Training Reporter, 20*(30), 883.

Cohen, M. (1988). *Restructuring the education system: Agenda for the 1990s.* Washington, DC: National Governor's Association.

Designs for Change. (1988). *Highlights of the Chicago School Reform Act.* Chicago: Author.

Edna McConnell Clark Foundation. (1988, October 31). *The Edna McConnell Clark Foundation Program for Disadvantaged Youth: Middle Grades Initiative.* New York: Author.

Education Commission of the States. (1988). *School reform in 10 states.* Denver, CO: Author.

Elmore, R.F., & McLaughlin, M.A. (1988, February). *Steady work: Policy, practice, and the reform of American education.* Santa Monica, CA: The RAND Corporation.

Hill, P.T., Wise, A.E., & Shapiro, L. (1989, January). *Educational progress: Cities mobilize to improve their schools.* Santa Monica, CA: The RAND Corporation.

Mizell, H., & Fleming, W. (1988, November 7). *Memorandum on overview and guidelines for submission of proposals.* New York: Edna McConnell Clark Foundation.

National Foundation for the Improvement of Education. (1988, June). *NFIE announces: Preparing disadvantaged young adolescents for the twenty-first century: High expectations, high content, high support.* Washington, DC: Author.

Renz, L. (1989). *Foundations today: Current facts and figures on private and community foundations* (6th ed.). New York: The Foundation Center.

Part II
Families and Communities

4

Critical Factors in Why Disadvantaged Students Succeed or Fail in School

Reginald M. Clark

I want to share with you a perspective on the education of the disadvantaged child that will hopefully stimulate discussion. I have been working in the area of children's learning and schooling processes for about 15 years. I started doing research on these topics around 1973 as a graduate student at Wisconsin, first in Chicago with Black twelfth graders, and later looking at Hispanic, White, Black, and Asian elementary, middle, and high school youngsters in Los Angeles. Initially, I was studying small groups of youngsters with regard to their family and community experiences. More recently I have been working within the Los Angeles Unified School District to analyze data obtained from several thousand youngsters, exploring the statistical relationships between variables and the implications of some of these correlations.

What I hope to do in the time I have with you this morning is to provide a perspective on two issues or questions. The first is "how do youngsters learn?" and, the second, "why do some youngsters who live in 'disadvantaged' social circumstances succeed, while other youngsters who come from the same social circumstances fail?" If we need to define "disadvantaged circumstances," "at-risk circumstances," or what it means to be "at risk for educational failure," we could come up with a variety of definitions for these terms.

Traditional sociological and sociopsychological research theories have held that a person is disadvantaged to the degree that he or she can be categorized or typed as belonging to a minority group, a low-income group, or a group with low educational and occupational status, or as living in a community that is considered to be unhealthy to well-being—for example, where the crime rate is high, and where the local schools do not provide the mix of resources that are necessary for educational and occupational success.

Similarly, a person could be from an upper-middle-class background and have parents who have access to huge sums of money and have "everything going for them" in an external sense, yet suffer from low self-esteem, which restricts the child from enjoying those advantages. That person, too, may be educationally or attitudinally disadvantaged.

Perhaps this is sufficient definition, although we might indeed come up with some other definitions of disadvantaged, based on a person's values and attitudes, for example. We might ultimately discover that educational disadvantaged might be most appropriately defined as the lack of any one of the necessary and sufficient conditions for educational success and/or occupational success. So perhaps after we think it through and come to some clearer understanding about what those conditions for success are, we can then examine whether a particular population has acquired them. We might say that a person or a group is, in fact, disadvantaged to the extent it appears not to have acquired the necessary and sufficient conditions for success.

My research has helped to confirm the hypothesis that who gets ahead in the schools is not predicted or explained by social background circumstances. However, social background circumstances clearly have shown a moderate statistical correlation to school achievement in other studies on this subject. Of the many studies that have shown a statistical correlation between background, life chances, and life achievements, few seem to adequately explain the fact that despite disadvantages of social background, many youngsters perform very well in school and in later life.

If you tuned into the Democratic presidential nomination process in Atlanta, you heard one of the candidates give his "where I came from" speech. He pointed out that he had come from a set of social circumstances that, according to experts, would have deemed him a strong candidate for failure. And yet he had not failed. Indeed, if it were true that background circumstances explained individual success or failure, then Black people would all still be in slavery, since almost all American Black people were slaves less than 125 years ago. Yet, numerous Blacks have come out of that condition and have achieved in school and in life. So the question of how to account for their achievements in the face of their adverse circumstances seems to me to be an important one.

I would argue that contextual factors probably are important for identifying populations most likely to be at risk of not succeeding in school. (We can identify low-income and minority populations as most likely not to succeed.) However, we should not infer that those social background characteristics are the reason why such persons do not succeed.

Conceptually, we can think of a person's social circumstances as represented by a large circle. These circumstances or conditions circumscribe the range of options for learning. Within that circle there is an inner circle, which we can call school achievements or life achievements. Between the outer circle and the inner circle is a variety of behaviors and attitudes that transform the inner circle (what is achieved). In other words, social circumstances do not have an independent effect on life achievements. Rather, their effect (if any) is mediated by other behavioral and attitudinal variables—variables sometimes referred to as cultural and process factors or developmental-ecological factors.

Basically, at various stages in a child's life—during the preschool years, the early primary years, the middle-school years, the junior high years, the high school years, and beyond—certain kinds of behaviors and attitudes characterize a person's life experience. It is these behaviors and attitudes that will determine how much and what the youngster learns.

Achievement is best understood as the result of interpersonal communication in everyday life, and this communication occurs in a variety of ecological contexts—the home, the school, the neighborhood, and other community institutions like churches, recreation centers, libraries, museums, tutorial centers, grocery stores, and playgrounds—that naturally occur in the lives of many children.

The environments and settings I have researched fairly extensively are the home and the neighborhood. I have discovered that we can more accurately predict a youngster's success or failure in school by finding out whether or not he or she typically spends approximately 20 to 35 hours a week (of the 60 to 70 waking hours a week that are available to a youngster) engaging in what I call constructive learning activity. In a given week, this would consist of 4 or 5 hours of discussion with knowledgeable adults or peers, 4 or 5 hours of leisure reading, 1 or 2 hours of writing of various types (whether writing grocery lists, writing in a diary, taking messages on the telephone, or writing letters), 5 or 6 hours of homework, several hours devoted to hobbies, 2 or 3 hours of chores, 4 or 5 hours of games (certain kinds of games in particular, like Monopoly and Scrabble and Dominoes, that require the player to read, spell, write, compute, solve problems, make decisions, and use other cognitive skills and talents transferable to school lessons). This constructive learning activity also includes exposure to cultural activities, theater, movies, and sports.

Table 4.1 presents typical activity schedules for achieving youngsters. These schedules depict the wide variety of constructive learning activities such youngsters participate in outside of school.

These various experiences create opportunities for youngsters to extend their practice of the very cognitive skills that schools want to teach. The reason that youngsters who do these things outside of school are more likely to be achievers is because they receive appropriately rich opportunities to extend their learning within a well-rounded array of activity contexts.

In contrast, youngsters who do not get the opportunity to participate in the appropriate amounts of these kinds of activities tend not to get the same mental workout. They do not get the cognitive exposure that seems to be essential to perform effectively in school classrooms and on standardized tests in reading, English, language arts, math, history, social studies, science, and other subject areas.

So what we are talking about on one level is discovering, and in fact ensuring, that youngsters get the appropriate level of exposure to acts of reading, writing, computation, listening, speaking, and problem-solving while participating in various cultural, intellectual, artistic, recreational and religious rituals, games, and hobbies. This, it seems to me, is the essence of the educator's problem. How do we find ways to ensure that the overall life experience of all youngsters is sufficiently rich so as to guarantee their academic competitiveness and competence in the subjects the schools want to teach?

An article in *Reaching for Excellence: An Effective Schools Sourcebook*, Kyle (1985) provides an excellent summary of research on effective elementary classroom practices. One of the tables in the

Table 4.1.   Some Typical 3 p.m.–9 p.m. Activity Schedules for Achieving 10-Year-Olds*

- Have snack, do homework, play or TV, help mom with dinner and clean up (talk time), hobby (model planes) or TV, reading, bed.

- Attend after-school lessons (music, drama, discussion group, tutoring) dinner, homework, talk or play or errands, TV with family, game or read, bath, bed.

- Go to grandfather's (and talk), swim, help mom with dinner (and talk), homework, games, bed.

- Chores, play, read or homework, sign language class, discuss class with parents, TV, prepare for next day.

- Homework, snack, baseball practice, dinner and clean up, TV, talk or read, bed.

---

*Los Angeles Study

Table 4.1. (Cont'd.)   Some Typical 3 p.m.–9 p.m. Activity Schedules for
Achieving 18-Year-Olds*

- Go to school club meetings, care for infant offspring, homework, dinner, talk about
  topical issues with family, talk on phone or see friends, read, bed.

- Play chess at school, come home and talk with mom, eat, play guitar or go out to
  play ball, do homework or read, bed.

- Participate in school sports (wrestling, track) and school clubs (Spanish Club, college
  algebra enrichment class, NCCJ club, etc.), homework or TV or talk with mom and
  brother, bed.

- Come home and rest, watch TV, do homework, dinner, dishes and chores, read or
  study, talk with mom and older sister, watch some TV and play educational games,
  bed.

*Chicago Study

article pertains to estimates of students' learning time during the
school day and school year (Stallings, 1985).

The table breaks down how much academic learning time is typical
in American classrooms, how much time students are actually engaged in learning versus instructional time, allocated time, attendance time, and total available time. For our purposes here, I will just
talk about engaged time. Engaged time is the amount of time that a
student is actually on task, doing cognitive work related to acts of
reading, writing, oral communication, test taking, and so on. When a
student is engaged, that youngster is actively thinking about or doing
the activity.

Students spend between 1.5 and 3.5 hours a day reading, computing,
writing, problem solving, and otherwise cogitating in a typical school
classroom. If you tease that out further, a youngster is engaged about
300–700 hours per year in the processes of learning in the typical
public school classroom. Some students are getting up to an additional
400 hours per year to practice these essential skills in the school
setting. This represents up to 114 percent more time spent on task. At
this rate, by the end of fifth grade high-achieving youngsters will have
engaged in the learning process at school as much as or more than low-
achieving tenth graders.

Apparently, 300 hours per year is not enough time to learn everything that schools want to teach. The average youngster simply won't
learn it all in that amount of time. Therefore, more opportunities are
required. (I am not the only one who has made this assertion.
Benjamin Bloom [1976] who has been doing research on this topic for
many years, discusses this in some detail in his book, *Human
Characteristics and School Learning*, and in other books he has
written since then.)

Table 4.2.   Categories of Common Activities Among American Children
(operable at each stage of the life course)

1. Professionally guided, formal learning activities

2. Deliberate out-of-school learning and work activities

3. High-yield leisure activities

4. Recreational activities

5. Health maintenance activities

Where are those requisite opportunities typically found? In experiences that occur away from school, in the home and community, and during evenings, weekends, summer months, and school vacations. Our research is helping us to better understand the connection between what happens in school and what youngsters do away from school, and how students' total array of behaviors in these contexts shapes success or failure in the learning process.

There are five categories of activity that allow youngsters opportunities to engage in stimulating cognitive work. Table 4.2 presents these categories of activity.

Professionally guided, formal academic learning activities such as classroom lessons and tutorials geared toward personal and intellectual growth are a major category of activity. What happens in school classes is critical to academic performance on standardized tests. Youngsters in less challenging classrooms will spend approximately 7.5 hours a week engaged in learning, while youngsters in better organized classrooms will spend closer to 17.5 hours a week engaged in the process of learning.

There are other differences in learning opportunities at the level of the classroom, not only in terms of time on task, but also in terms of curricular content and instructional process. We can document differences in youngsters' experiences across various classrooms and within different groups of youngsters in the same classroom. If there is tracking or an ability-grouping system of classroom management, some youngsters may be on task for 7.5 hours a week, and others in the same class may be on task for 17.5 hours a week simply because of the way the classroom is organized.

So classroom activity is one component of learning opportunity. Beyond the classroom, successful youngsters are more likely to engage in a well-rounded, balanced array of activities than are less successful youngsters whose lifestyles tend to reflect imbalanced time-use patterns.

Deliberate out-of-school learning and work activities are a second major category of activity that provides opportunities for cognitive work. Homework, study, after-school lessons, independent tutorials, part-time work, learning how to play an instrument, and learning a new language such as Spanish or French are examples of this kind of activity.

A third category consists of high-yield leisure activities. I say "high yield" because these activities normally provide a high amount of opportunity for youngsters to practice acts of reading, writing, discussing, problem solving, decision making, and so on. They are "leisure" in the sense that they are done for fun. Reading a book for fun is one example. Talking with parents about the political elections, about why it is important to get an education, or about ways of successfully handling a problematic job situation offers another example. Participating in organized youth programs (e.g., Scouts) and summer camps or visiting museums are further examples.

A fourth category is that of recreational activities—watching television, playing games, listening to music, doing hobbies, observing or participating in group sports, playing outside, hanging out, partying, skipping rope, going on nature hikes or family vacations, and so on.

The fifth category consists of what I describe as health maintenance activities—emotional, mental, and physical health—which include everything from going to church, praying or meditating, eating, daydreaming or sleeping, washing and grooming oneself, or doing physical conditioning exercises.

This framework or schema of contexts for learning seems to capture many typical activities in the lives of all American youngsters, regardless of their gender, race, or social class background. Achieving youths tend to pursue an activity pattern that is wholesome, nurturing, and balanced in the sense that these youngsters spend approximately 20 to 35 hours a week or more doing various high-yield leisure and deliberate learning activities. The rest of their out-of-school time is spent doing health maintenance and recreational activities. In addition, they spend time learning in better organized classrooms each week.

Underachieving youngsters typically spend less time attending school; that is, they attend school less often. Even when they go to school regularly, they are likely to be in classrooms where students spend less time learning—7.5 hours a week engaged in the learning process in comparison to the 17.5 hours that students get in the better organized classes. They are likely, also, to spend much less time engaged in deliberate learning and work or high-yield leisure activities. They spend time in recreational activities, watching TV and videos, playing the record player, listening to music on the radio, and other kinds of "hanging out" activities.

In fact, their activity schedule is top-heavy with that kind of thing. We might compare it to having an imbalanced food diet, a diet that consists largely of Twinkies and candy (recreational activities) versus a balanced diet which includes vegetables, protein products, and all proper vitamins as well (deliberate learning/high-yield leisure activities). Low-achieving youngsters have a diet that has lots of candy, cake, and cookies in it. And we all know what happens if you continually eat a lot of cake, cookies, and candies and not enough of the grains, fruits, and protein-rich products. You tend to get physically sick. Your immune system is affected negatively.

As with the research of Benjamin Bloom (1976, 1981), Herbert Walberg (1984a, 1984b), and others (Grave, Weinstein, & Walberg, 1983) who have done case study analyses and metaanalyses of thousands of studies, my studies show that youngsters who are academically successful tend to have greater opportunity to participate in a well-rounded, balanced diet of activities.

There are a number of process factors that shape the impact of this well-rounded schedule on students. I developed a four-element paradigm of these activity patterns. These four elements compose the learning opportunity structure. The first two elements are closely related: time spent on a particular learning task as well as the amount of opportunity the child has to become actively involved in acts of cogitation while engaged in that task. The third element is the extent of input by knowledgeable adults. And the fourth element has to do with the hidden (or not so hidden) rules, standards, expectations, and goals for the activity that surround it as it occurs. A student's activity diet not only must include an array of wholesome activities; it also must become a routine, almost a ritual, in the student's life. Further, teaching and learning must proceed in ways that help the student become firm and automatic in the use of basic literacy skills. For optimal literacy skills acquisition to occur, the quality of the material that the youngster is reading must be sufficiently interesting and challenging. It is one thing for a student to read children's novels and comic books about science fiction topics that are stimulating; it is another thing entirely to spend an hour going over two pages of a second grade "see Dick run" type of book when the youngster is in the fifth grade. Different information is provided by these two qualities of reading content.

Other activities need to include opportunities for the student to acquire regular, high-quality instruction. That is, youngsters need to obtain an adequate level of support, feedback, and help from knowledgeable adults and peers during an activity. For example, being able to interact with a knowledgeable parent or peer about what a youngster has read would give the youngster opportunities for support and feedback during the reading activity.

In addition to this paradigm to help us see why some youngsters succeed and others fail, I think we need to be cognizant of other factors at all times. It is important to examine (within the context of the home, school, and community) what kinds of adult modeling occur. What does the youngster see other adults do, especially other adults who are significant to that youngster (adults about whom the youngster has strong feelings, either positive or negative)? What kinds of exposure is that youngster getting through significant others? What kinds of media images are being modeled to the youngsters?

Sentiments and feelings also should be analyzed. During the various activities that occur in the home, school, and community institutions, what kinds of feelings/affects permeate the various experiences? How do these feelings affect the students' motivation?

I have made an attempt in my research to operationalize the concept of love (which is, of course, probably an impossible task). The yardsticks I use involve the ways in which youngsters get nurtured and named—the extent to which they get actual physical hugs or are shown in various other ways that they are respected and cared about.

In one pilot study we did in Los Angeles, we looked at family sharing and labeling as indicators of love. The parents of academically successful youngsters were more likely to share personal problems with their children and nurture them when they were feeling down. This was reciprocal. The youngsters would in fact nurture the parents. Together they would do things—they performed rituals like braiding the hair or rubbing the scalp or massaging the skin or eating ice cream together—nurturing behaviors that reflected loving feelings.

Also, parents had labeled their successful children in ways that were endearing. For example, the parents of achieving youngsters frequently had given them nicknames that reflected a positive role definition. For example, they assigned their children names like "Tiger" or "Wizard," or they would say, "He's my smart one." Or, "She always does things the way I want her to do them. I can always depend on her. Whatever I ask her to do, when I come home, I know it is going to be done." Or, "He can really make it as long as he puts his mind to it."

In the homes of the less successful youngsters, there was a tendency for these behaviors to be lacking. For example, it was less likely that the parent and child shared information and nurtured one another. These youngsters were less likely to have been assigned positive, endearing nicknames. Frequently they answered to unflattering names like "Snake," "Fatso," "Dumbbell," "Half-pint," "Stuff," "Stinky," and so on.

When the interviewers asked, "Why do you call the child by that name?" parents always claimed something like, "Well, I don't mean anything by it; that's what we've called him since he was a baby." When parents described such youngsters, they frequently would add, "He has always had trouble," or, "She just really is slow, you know," and, "I could tell when she was two months old that she is like her father— ornery." "I could tell when she was two days old she had this kind of personality."

And you can't convince the parents otherwise. They "saw it." The question in my mind is, "Which came first, the chicken or the egg?" Did they "see" a particular personality? Was it actually there? Or did they create it? I believe that personality patterns are largely created by parental actions. If the child showed a predisposition toward a certain personality, it certainly was reinforced by parental actions.

I am not suggesting that because a youngster has an unflattering nickname, he of she is going to be an underachiever. I am merely suggesting that labels are often a clue to deeper perceptions about the youngster and about what the youngster is capable of doing.

The mother's attitude about her youngster sometimes was driven by her attitude about the child's father. If the children in a household had different fathers, the mother may have given more quality time to the youngster whose father had treated her relatively well over her other child whose father had abused her. Affective, psychosocial dynamics in the home impacted what roles parents assigned to their youngsters early on. These role assignments defined their personalities to a large extent.

In addition, it is important to identify and assess the norms, standards, rules, and expectations that permeate the various contexts of the home, the school, and the community. To what degree are they encouraging the development of an academic work ethic and academic success?

I am reminded of some households in which there was an implicit expectation for teen pregnancy. Parents would say, on the one hand, "I don't want my girl to get pregnant until she gets married," while at the same time engaging in what I would call enabling behavior that sent mixed messages to the youngster and in fact gave her the idea that "maybe it is all right if I go out and get pregnant, because Mom has said, 'Girl, if you do bring a baby in here, I am going to take care of it,' and in other ways she's suggested that maybe it wouldn't be that bad if it happened to me."

Looking very closely at these rules, standards, norms, and expectations is critical. What are the attitudes and the relationships between youngsters and their parents, relatives, teachers, ministers, coaches, instructors, and tutors in community programs, and so forth?

These are some of the critical elements that I think need to be considered within the activity schema. I think that these activities and related elements need to be considered for children at different points over their lifecycle. How did this system of factors look during preschool (ages two, three, and four), how did it look when the youngster was seven or eight years old, when the youngster was ten or eleven years old, and so forth? You might find pattern differences or pattern consistencies.

I suspect that the youngsters who achieve most highly will show a pattern consistency in constructive learning over the life stages. As Benjamin Bloom has found in his studies, youngsters who come closest to reaching the limits of their learning potential (highly rated research mathematicians, neurologists, pianists, tennis players, swimmers, and others) show a certain common pattern in their lives.

By the time they were five or six years old, they were doing the activity they were expert at (or some aspect of it) in a "just for fun" kind of way. By the time they were seven or eight, they were getting tutorial help to enhance their skill, frequently from a professional who knew more than the parent about it. By the time they were 11 or 12, they were doing it with professional help on a regular basis, usually about 35 or 40 hours a week or more—as much time as the average adult works in a given week. These youngsters were doing the activity more than anybody else. This is why they were doing it better than others.

I will conclude with a little citation from scripture. As pointed out in the Bible, in James, second chapter, 26th verse, "For as the body without the spirit is dead, so faith without works is dead also."

Research studies have shown that disadvantaged youngsters have positive attitudes about themselves and about academic achievement. Yet they don't do the work that it takes to ensure the outcome of high achievement. Our challenge as educators, it seems to me, is to figure out ways to systematically ensure that these youngsters will have opportunities to do the necessary cognitive work during activities that stimulate and challenge their minds.

REFERENCES

Bloom, B.S. (1976). *Human characteristics and school learning*. New York: McGraw-Hill.

Bloom, B.S. (1981). *All our children learning*. New York: McGraw-Hill.

Grave, M.E., Weinstein, T., & Walberg, H.J. (1983). School-based home instruction and learning: A quantitative synthesis. *Journal of Educational Research, 76*, 351-360.

Kyle, R.M.J. (1985). *Reaching for excellence: An effective schools sourcebook.* Washington, DC: U.S. Department of Education.

Stallings, J. (1985). Effective elementary classroom practices. In R.M.J. Kyle (Ed.), *Reaching for excellence.* Washington, DC: U.S. Department of Education.

Walberg, H.J. (1984a). Families as partners in educational productivity. *Phi Delta Kappan, 65*, 397-400.

Walberg, H.J. (1984b). Improving productivity in America's schools. *Educational Leadership, 41*, 19-27.

ADDITIONAL REFERENCES

Becker, H. (1952). Social class variations in teacher-pupil relationships. *Journal of Educational Sociology, 25*, 451–465.

Bowles, S., & Gintis, H. (1976). *Schooling in capitalist America.* New York: Basic Books.

Clark, R. (1983). *Family life and school achievement.* Chicago: University of Chicago Press.

Clark, R. (1988). *Critical factors in why disadvantaged students succeed or fail in school.* Washington, DC: Academy for Educational Development.

Comer, J.P. (1986, February). Parent participation in the schools. *Phi Delta Kappan, 67*, 442-446.

Dave, R.H. (1963). *The identification and measurement of environmental process variables that are related to educational achievement.* Doctoral dissertation, University of Chicago.

DiPrete, T.A. (1981). *Discipline, order and student behavior in American high schools* (ERIC Document: ED 224137). Chicago: National Opinion Research Center.

Dreeben, R. (1968). *On what is learned in school.* Reading, MA: Addison Wesley.

Epstein, J.L. (1987, February). Parent involvement. *Education and Urban Society, 19*, 119-136.

Getzels, J.W. (1974, December). Socialization and education: A note on discontinuities. *Teachers College Record, 76*, 218-225.

Gray, S.T. (1984). How to create a successful school-community partnership, *Phi Delat Kappan, 65*, 405-409.

Hale-Benson, J.E. (1982). *Black children.* Baltimore: Johns Hopkins University Press.

Hansen, D.A. (1986). Family-school articulations: The effects of interaction rule mismatch. *American Educational Research Journal, 23*, 643-659.

Henderson, A. (1987). *The evidence continues to grow.* Columbia, MD: National Committee for Citizens in Education.

Hoover-Dempsey, K.V., Bassler, O.C., & Brissie, J.S. (1987). Parent involvement: Contributions of teacher efficacy, school SES, and other school characteristics. *American Educational Research Journal, 24,* 417-435.

Johnston, J.H. (1986, March). *Dimensions of family participation in the life of schools.* Paper presented to the annual convention of the National Association of Secondary School Principals, Orlando, FL.

Lareau, A. (1987, April). Social class differences in family school relationships. *Sociology of Education, 60,* 73-85.

Leacock, E.B. (1969). *Teaching and learning in city schools.* New York: Basic Books.

Lewis, H. (1967). The changing negro family. In J. Roberts (Ed.), *School children in the urban slum.* New York: The Free Press.

Lightfoot, S.L. (1978). *Worlds apart: Relationships between families and schools.* New York: Basic Books.

Lightfoot, S.L., & Carew, J.V. (1974). *Individuation and discrimination in the classroom.* Washington, DC: Child Development Associates, Inc., Office of Child Development.

McPherson, G. (1972). *Small town teacher.* Cambridge, MA: Harvard University Press.

Ogbu, J. (1974). *The next generation.* New York: Academic Press.

Slater, P. (1968). Social change in the democratic family. In Bennis & Slater (Ed.), *The temporary society.* New York: Harper and Row.

Topping, K.J. (1986). *Parents as educators.* Cambridge, MA: Brookline Books.

Walberg, H.J. (1984a). Families as partners in educational productivity. *Phi Delta Kappan, 65,* 397-400.

Walberg, H.J. (1984b). Improving the productivity of America's schools. *Educational Leadership, 41,* 19-27.

Warren, R. (1973). The classroom as sanctuary for teachers: Discontinuity and social control. *American Anthropologist, 75,* 280-291.

Weiss, J. (1969). *The identification and measurement of environmental process variables related to self-esteem.* Doctoral dissertation, University of Chicago.

Wilson, W.J. (1987). *The truly disadvantaged.* Chicago: University of Chicago Press.

Wolf, R.H. (1964). *The identification and measurement of environmental process variables related to intelligence.* Doctoral dissertation, University of Chicago.

5
Mediating School Cultural Knowledge For Children: The Parent's Role

Concha Delgado-Gaitan
Martha Allexsaht-Snider

Research has clearly revealed that parental involvement in their children's education enhances the opportunity for academic success. The home environment has been identified as the primary learning environment, particularly in the early childhood years (Comer, 1984). According to Comer, the parents and extended family networks guide children through increasingly complex intellectual tasks, which are facilitated through the attachment process. Children internalize the experiences of the household as they develop a sense of belonging, worth, and identity.

Learning in the home is influenced by a variety of characteristics including education and income levels of the parents. Family behaviors, such as whether parents read to children and enforce rules about homework and television, also shape the home learning environments. Family patterns, marital status, parents' educational experience, employment, and social support networks all help to explain the family's ability to relate to the school. Furthermore, family attitudes, such as parental expectations and the child's self-esteem, provide an emotional framework for the children's home learning environment.

When children enter preschool, they bring with them their cultural mapping which enables them to perform in culturally appropriate ways. When family culture and or social class differs from that of the school, conflicts may arise for the children in their academic and social adjustment giving rise to preschool family intervention programs. Many programs have been instituted to shape the child to the model of the school, and the programs have yielded positive gains. Bronfenbrenner (1974a) demonstrated that mothers who received training in how to stimulate verbal interaction with their children helped their children achieve better in school.

Gotts (1980) examined longitudinal effects (5-year) on Appalachian preschool children ages 3–5 whose parents had been trained in their home on a weekly visit by paraprofessionals to augment daily lessons broadcasted on television. The experimental group showed consistently higher achievement on the Appalachian Preschool Frostig Test of Visual Perception and the Peabody Picture Vocabulary Test through the first five years of their schooling as compared to the control group children who received only television lessons without augmented activities. Becher (1984) later confirmed the success of training parents to work with their children. The author documented that in school-based programs where low socioeconomic parents have been trained to work with their children, significant academic improvement on the part of the students ensued.

In preschool programs whose families participated actively, children did better in school than comparable children whose parents did not participate. The effects have been studied for as long as 10 years after the children left the preschool program. One such longitudinal study of 11 early childhood projects confirmed the long-term effects on children of parents who actively participated in their preschool education (Lazar & Darlington, 1978). The children of active parents had significantly fewer assignments to special education and fewer grade retentions than the control group as children moved up into the upper grades.

An experimental study in New York by Irvine (1979) also concluded that the amount of time spent by low working-class parents with their preschool children was related to student achievement. Four levels of involvement were determined according to the number of hours (50, 100, 150, 200 hours) the parents were involved over the school year. School-related knowledge and skills as measured by the Cooperative Preschool Inventory and the Peabody Picture Vocabulary Test showed a highly significant relationship between parent involvement and achievement, with the greatest gains made by children who initially had the lowest scores.

Parent involvement has also been found crucial to children's social and academic success as the children move into higher grades. Parent involvement components in the schools have been studied (Gordon, 1978; Herman & Yeh, 1980; Irvine, 1979) to understand parents' impact on the school and indirectly on their children's achievement. A variety of conditions were found in homes whose children were said to be "at risk" academically in upper elementary grades. These children often excelled in school once their parents received training in home teaching techniques (Boulder Valley, Colorado School District, 1975; Bronfenbrenner, 1974a, 1974b; Delgado-Gaitan, 1990; Gotts, 1980; Lazar & Darlington, 1978). As children began to experience difficulty in school, research indicated that parent education techniques to train parents to assist children at home yielded rewarding results for the children (Karraker, 1972). These studies stress convincingly that parents must encourage their children to talk about books they read, must converse with their children about school, and practice school-like curriculum including colors, letters, and math concepts in the early school grades.

In his case study of ten black high school students and their families, Clark (1983) concluded that certain patterns in a family's overall cultural style, not marital status, education level, income, or social surroundings, determined whether children were prepared for competent performance in school. Families that incorporated frequent dialogue between parents and children and were warm and supportive toward their children, yet set clear and consistent limits, had students who were high achievers. The fact that these families were also single-parent families, of low socioeconomic or educational levels, was not significant. The parents of successful students held common attitudes toward the importance of education and they consistently put children's needs before their own.

Most studies on parent involvement reveal its critical nature to academic achievement thus substantiating school interventions in the home. While it is important for children to achieve in school, Revicki (1981) and later Cochran and Henderson (1986) confirmed that part of parent involvement implies congruent home and school learning environments through school-designed interventions. That is, not only is the family influenced by the school, but the school is also influenced by the family. This presumes sociocultural change for both the family and the school. Just as schools intervene to teach the family about the school rules and expectations, so do schools need to incorporate families in different activities that accommodate the parents' work hours and their varying degrees of knowledge about the school.

While abundant research exists on preschool and early childhood schooling, limited research exists on programs for parents of older students such as the Follow Through Program which has been a good example of high student, school, and community impact through parent involvement. The Follow Through Program is a national effort designed to have counselors based at an institution of higher education to assist junior high and high school students through daily tutoring. Summer intensive course, family resources, and counseling are also provided. Gordon (1978) shows that the more comprehensive and longlasting the parent involvement activity, the more likely its effectiveness.

Longer-lasting effects on first-grade tests for children whose parents had received both school and home training on specific enrichment activities were revealed in an experimental study in the Boulder Valley, Colorado, School District (1975). Researchers documented the fact that academically high-risk kindergarten children in the experimental group scored higher on first-grade standardized tests when their parents received teacher-designed, parent–child home training, than did high-risk children in the control group who participated only in an in-school enhancement program.

The Washington, D.C. School District demonstrated positive effects on achievement in an elementary school program serving low-income students in a segregated setting studied by Gross, Ridgley, and Gross (1974). A comprehensive development program for staff, parents, and community members included a community development component as well as in-service programs for the teachers. Parents were trained through workshops and continuing education classes in areas such as health and consumer education. Parents also attended family counseling services weekly. Ultimately, students gained in personal and academic development if their families emphasize schooling in every way possible during the students' school career as Epstein (1987) concluded.

The gains of parent involvement are for the students' attitudes about themselves and their control over their environment which are critical factors in achievement (Bronfenbrenner, 1979; Tizard, Schofield, & Hewison, 1982). When parents show interest in their children's learning (which is congruent with the expectations of the school), children's academic performance usually increases.

MEDIATION IN THE SOCIAL CONTEXT

While research studies have concluded that diverse parental involvement in the schools and in the homes enhances student achievement, most of these studies have focused on achievement outcomes as opposed to the process of parental involvement. Absent in the research is the sociocultural perspective examining how the process of parental involvement functions in an interactive context between parents and children. That is, how do parents transmit their knowledge about the schooling process to children, and how do children reflect that knowledge in actions that transform their schooling experience?

The answer to this question is premised on the understanding of sociocultural transmission of knowledge in a social context. Theories on how this process occurs have been advanced by social psychologists, among them Feuerstein (1980), who brings a psychological rather than a sociocultural perspective to the examination of parent/child interactions. His work with parents and other caregivers as mediators of children's learning experiments merits consideration because it elucidates the process of mediation in parent involvement.

In Feuerstein's conceptual framework, adults in a child's life who can effectively focus attention and interpret to her the significance of objects, events, and ideas in her social context are instrumental in the child's development of an ability to learn and solve problems. The parent or the other adult, guided by her own intentions, culture, and emotional investment, selects and organizes the experiences and stimuli for the child. "The mediator selects stimuli that are most appropriate and then frames, filters and schedules them.... Through this process of mediation, the cognitive structure of the child is affected. The child acquires behavior patterns and learning sets..." (Feuerstein, 1980, p. 16). Mediation, however, does not exist in isolation from family's the social environment. It must be examined, as we attempted to do in this study, in children's interactions with their parents and their teachers as well as the interactions between teachers and parents regarding the children.

The fundamental meaning of mediation relative to learning has been proposed in the work of Neo-Vygotskians (see Cole, Gay, Glick, & Sharp, 1971; Diaz, Moll, & Mehan, 1986; Trueba, 1989) who have advanced Vygotsky's (1978) theory of child development. They have studied the components of the social learning environment that encourage learning. People in interaction with each other constitute social environments in which people learn by working within their "zone of proximal development" (ZPD), a concept explaining child development (Vygotsky, 1978). The importance of parental mediations in the children's schooling activities lies in the potential learning which occurs under adult guidance. Vygotsky proposed the zone of proximal development to explain the essence of learning under guidance. His definition was *the distance between the actual development level as determined by independent problem solving and the level of potential development as determined through problem solving under adult guidance or in collaboration with more capable peers (p. 86)*. In practice, the interaction between children and adults may or may not move children through their zone of proximal development. Whether it does or not depends on the nature of the context. Success in moving children into their zone of proximal development is determined by how knowledgeable the adult is about the child and about the problem.

In this study, we examined the process of parental mediation with their children. We attempted to show that when adults were knowledgeable about the school system, they were more capable of mediating their children through school-related problems from an ecological perspective where the well-being of individuals are intimately connected to and affected by the environment in which people live (Bronfrenbrenner, 1979). It followed that when parents mediated their children through problems, children became more capable of functioning in their social environment. What was this cultural knowledge transmitted in the mediation process? The answer is revealed in the subsequent sections that describe interactions that led to motivation, social adjustment, and cognitive skill development of children through school.

THE STUDY

In 1985 we began a study which examined the social context of the parents' role in the academic socialization of Mexican-American children. The children were in different reading groups in a third-grade classroom. The study focused on early home patterns of socialization to school. We studied closely 12 families that had been selected as the most active parents in the class. They were identified as particularly motivated by examining the record of their second-grade involvement in a larger study.

Setting

Four elementary schools, one junior high school, and one high school comprise the Portillo School District. This study was conducted in the Marina Elementary School. The school is adjacent to a freeway exit, and is surrounded by a residential area comprised of single-family dwellings, a new condominium complex, and older, small apartments that serve as homes for large numbers of Mexican families whose children attend Marina School. Marina School's Mexican population is about 35 percent, and about 14 percent of the total student enrollment is limited-English-speaking. During the time of the study (1986–1987), the school was composed of second through sixth grades. A bilingual program exists at Marina and services the limited-English-speaking students. The Mexican population totals about 25 percent of the

Portillo community; less than 50 percent of them are limited-English-speaking. Although there are a few small industries in town including an aluminum factory and a shoe factory, nurseries constitute the major industry in Portillo. Numerous ranches surround the Portillo area, providing a source of employment for many Mexican men who do landscape work. Women also work, and their places of employment tend to be plant nurseries or housekeeping jobs in motels and ranches. The majority of the Mexican men and women are employed in the nurseries.

Working-class Mexican-American earn less than other groups (U.S. Census Bureau, 1981). In addition, soaring rents in the area have created a devastating financial burden for the families in our study as well as for others in the Portillo community. In 1987, the average family monthly income was less than $1300 despite both husband and wife (as well as other adults in the home) working full-time.

Mexican families in Portillo emigrated from different parts of Mexico (e.g., Guadalajara, Guerrero, Mexico City), major cities, and small towns in rural areas. Most Mexican people have lived in the Portillo area over 10 years, and have younger children born in the community. The average size of the Mexican working-class family is six, including the parents and children. Economic necessity has forced extended families to live together in small one or two-bedroom apartments. There are a few who live in small homes or on their own ranches on the outskirts of town, and some have bought one-room trailers.

Ethnographic data was collected from the 12 Mexican-American third grade students and their parents from Marina Elementary School in Portillo, California to answer the question: How do parents transmit knowledge of the schooling process to their children? The students and their families were observed and interviewed over a period of one year. The primary focus involved activities in which parents and children dealt with school-related issues.

A series of ethnographic interviews with parents determined the different ways in which they participated in their children's school life. Additionally, the interviews revealed the parental educational background and the motivation for involving themselves in the school. Parents discussed the nature of their children's school-related problems and their strategies for dealing with them.

Observations employing audiotapes and field notes recorded parent/child interactions in the home pertaining to school-related topics, and parental visits to school. Such interactions revealed the parental expectations for school behavior and achievement. Observations also included classroom teacher/student interactions and teacher/parent conferences.

Parent Socialization of Children

Mexican-American households in the study unanimously believed that education was important for their children, yet they differed in the type of involvement they had in their children's schooling. A few families participated in literacy activities with their children at home, but had minimal contact with the teacher (see Table 5.1 and Table 5.2).

Although some families communicated frequently with the teacher about their children's academic performance and held their children accountable for completing their academic tasks, they did not read to their children at home. Still other parents did not communicate frequently with teachers although they attempted to help their children in their school-related tasks because their children were, according to teachers' reports, underachieving in school.

DATA AND ANALYSIS

Motivation

Children's willingness to participate actively in their schooling has much to do with the home environment that stimulates and sustains their interest in school. Much of the motivation transmitted to children derived from the parents' belief that education could improve their children's future economic opportunities. Parents' interactions with their children demonstrated their ability to persuade them about the importance of school (see Table 5.2).

Parents differed in the approaches they used to motivate their children. Some parents talked to their children about the importance of schooling in the context of discussing school reports from the teacher. Other parents made it a point to weave in the need for education and schooling when they related stories about their life in Mexico to their children. The message was conveyed strongly, although children usually listened without much response, as parents encouraged them to do their best in school. Mrs. Cortina tells of her conversations with Irene who had always liked school, but on occasion she got into conflicts with her teacher or classmates that discouraged her. As a result she was reluctant to go to school as Mrs. Cortina tell:

> Yo le digo a mi hija que no debe de decepcionarse con problemas que tiene en la escuela. A veces la maestra trata de discipliner a Irene pero Irene se siente muy mal porque dice que la maestra no la quiere. Me dice que no quiere ir a la escuela porque la maestra la maltrata y no le hace nada a los otros niños. Yo he hablado con la maestra y me asegura que ella no maltrata a Irene y que también disciplina a los otros niños. Cuando Irene no quiere ir a la escuela yo le tengo que asegurar a ella la

Table 5.1.   Children in the Study

Name	Grade	Sex	Overall Classroom Academic Status	Siblings	Number of Parents in Home	Parents' Involvement in Child's Education
Maria Abeta	3	F	High	2	2	Active
Irene Cortine	3	F	High	3	2	Active
Yolanda Mendez	3	F	High	1	2	Active
Rosa Ortega	3	F	High	3	2	Active
Ramona Perez	3	F	Ave	2	1	Active
Sonia Sanchez	3	F	Ave	1	2	Active
Lupe Salinas*	3	F	Low	2	2	Active
Mario Barrera	3	M	High	3	2	Active
Beto Mata	3	M	High	2	2	Active
Raul Olivas	3	M	Ave	4	2	Active
Manuel Roble	3	M	Ave	2	2	Active
Pedro Zermeno	3	M	Ave	1	2	Active

*Lupe had improved her reading since the beginning of school year.

Table 5.2.   Parent Involvement in the Children's Schooling Activities

Name	Reading With Children at Home	Contacts With Teacher	Assistance With Homework
Maria Abeta	Y	Y	Y
Irene Cortina	Y	Y	Y
Yolanda Mendez	O	Y	Y
Rosa Ortega	O	O	Y
Ramona Perez	Y	Y	O
Sonia Sanchez	O	Y	O
Lupe Salinas	O	Y	O
Mario Barrera	Y	O	Y
Beto Mata	Y	O	Y
Raul Olivas	R	O	Y
Manuel Roble	O	Y	O
Pedro Zermeno	R	O	Y

CODE: Y = yes, consistently—daily or alternate day basis
O = occasionally, usually on a weekly basis
R = rarely, it has occurred irregularly
S = seldom—it was not a notable activity

importancia de estudiar ir a la escuela y que la maestra espera que se comporte bien para que aprenda. Yo creo que Irene me cree porque sabe que he hablado con su maestra.

I tell my daughter not to dispair with problems in school. Sometimes the teacher tries to discipline Irene and Irene feels bad because she says that the teacher doesn't like her. She tells me that she doesn't want to go to school because the teacher only punishes her and not the other kids. I've talked with the teacher and she assures me that she doesn't mistreat Irene and that she also disciplines the other children. When Irene does not want to go to school I have to assure her about the importance of going to school and that the teacher expects her to behave because it's for her own good. I think Irene believes me because she knows that I've talked with her teacher.

Another parent, Mrs. Olivas, related a different example of how motivation was transmitted to children. "Yo repaso todos los reportes que manda su maestra y casi siempre son buenos los reportes pero de vez en cuando son malos y yo me enojo con Beto." *I review all of my son's reports that the teacher sends and they're usually good but sometimes they're bad and I get mad at him.* Mrs. Olivas elaborated on the importance of schooling and commented on how she impresses the urgency of education on Beto. "Le digo que en México nosotros no podimos estudiar porque vivíamos muy lejos de la escuela en un rancho. Pero, ellos aquí tienen la oportunidad de estudiar gratis y deben de aprovechar todo lo que puedan." *I tell [Beto] that in Mexico we couldn't study because we lived too far away from the school in a ranch. But, here they have the opportunity to study free and they should take advantage of all they can.* This parent's words of encouragement rang true for many children whose parents did not have the opportunity to go to school. They were convinced, however, about the importance of schooling for their children.

When parents mediated their children's problems, they engaged them in understanding the nature of the conflict such that children were moved into their zone of proximal development by finding meaning in schooling and thus motivating themselves.

Social Adjustment

Education had a more profound meaning for most parents than simply sending their children to learn to read and write. To parents, the term "education"—*education*—meant that children should learn to be respectful, cooperative, and helpful to those around them. Parents expected their children to behave in school and to respect their teachers. Therefore, when parents learned that their children were not behaving at school, it did not matter to them if they were high achievers in their academic work, the children were reminded that they had broken a golden rule. Many parents realized that they had to communicate not only with their children at home but also with the teachers. While they trusted their children most of the time they believed that they should also let teachers know that it was just as important for them that their children behave respectfully as it was for them to achieve academically. Ramona's mother illustrates her concern and actions on behalf of her daughter's behavior in the following incident.

Mother: Mi hija, no me gusta este reporte de tu maestra. Por qué dice que tu no pones atención en la clase y que tienes que leer más en la casa? *Dear, I don't like this report from your teacher. Why does it say that you don't pay attention in class and that you need to read more at home?*

Ramona: No sé. *I don't know.*

Mother: Sabes que te he dicho que en la clase tienes que respetar a tu maestra porque ellas estan ahí para ayudarte. *You know that I've told you that to respect your teacher in class because they are there to help you.*

R: [Lowers her head and remains quiet.]

M: Mañana voy a hacer una cita con tu maestra para discutir este problema. *Tomorrow I'm going to make an appointment with your teacher to discuss this problem.*

Mrs. Perez sent a note to the teacher with Ramona and scheduled an appointment with her. In addition, Mrs. Perez called the school during her lunch break at work to confirm the after school appointment on that day.

Ramona was present at the meeting between the teacher and Mrs. Perez. The parent began by asking the teacher what the problem was with Ramona and why she received such a bad report. The teacher answered by saying that more than anything, Ramona had taken to talking too much to children around her and not finishing her assignments and that when the work went home it was not completed. Furthermore, because she is not completing her reading assignments she is in danger of falling behind in her work. Mrs. Perez turned to Ramona and asked her why she was behaving this way. Ramona lowered her head and in a quiet voice argued that the children around her talked to her and that it was not her fault. The teacher countered by saying that although others talked to her, she did not have to engage in conversation with them to the extent of neglecting her work. Ramona nodded affirmatively. Mrs. Perez reminded Ramona to do her work quietly and if any children around her tried to talk to her she needed to tell the teacher to move her. Essentially, they all agreed that Ramona could do her work if she could control her talking. Mrs. Perez also requested specific direction for reading with her at home to improve her reading. The teacher instructed Mrs. Perez to have

Ramona read the assignment aloud. The following week showed improvement in Ramona's behavior in the classroom but not without a challenge for her. In the classroom, Ramona tried to focus on her seat work while the teacher worked with other students. Occasionally, Ramona looked up to locate the teacher and continued doing her workbook. Although she did not initiate any conversation with other children, they sometimes asked her how to do the problem. Ramona responded in a low voice until she heard the teacher say, "Ramona, are you doing your wòrk?" Ramona responded "yes" then raised her hand. When the teacher got to Ramona, she told the teacher that the other children had initiated talk with her about the work pages. The teacher sat and talked to the four students in the group and stressed the need to be quiet while they worked so that they could complete their work.

At home, Ramona's mother asked her each day to report on how her classroom assignments were going, while reminding her to respect her teacher and to meet her teacher's expectations:

M: Ya sabes que aunque termines el trabajo en la clase tienes que leerme tu libro de tarea. *You know that even if you finish your work in class you still have to read your book to me for homework.*

R: Pero mamá, yo hago mi trabajo en clase. *But mom, I do my work in class.*

M: Yo sé, pero siempre tienes que leer aquí en la casa aunque no tengas tarea porque dice la maestra que es importante. *I know but you still have to read here at home because the teacher says it's important.*

The point is that the parent's active involvement with the child's schooling provided her with the support to deal with the day-to-day conflicts she faced—she knew that her mother expected her to do her best. The mother convinced Ramona that she could cooperate with the classroom rules as well as follow the family's values of respect for the teacher.

Parents believed that their children's behavior in the classroom represented a crucial aspect of their ability to learn. "Si pones atención, aprendes" *If you pay attention, you'll learn,* commented one parent. Parents also felt strongly that the children's behavior away from home reflected on the family' character and reputation and they mediated actively in shaping children's values accordingly. When the teacher's reports reflected children's good behavior, parents saw the success of their mediation to improve their children's social conduct in school. The insistence respectful behavior on the part of the family and the school represented congruence of this value. Parents, however, found that although their children were taught to respect adults in the school, they should also be assertive in expecting the children to behave respectfully them as well.

Cognitive Skills Development

Parents had a more difficult time in helping their children when they had to work with them on homework activities. Problems with homework nearly always meant frustrations for the parents as well as the students due to the nature of the academic work that students had to complete which challenged parents confidence in their own cognitive skills. Most of the parents had less than a sixth-grade education in Mexico, and although they had literacy skills in Spanish, they were unfamiliar with the American school curriculum. Parents mediated to the extent that they could understand the assignment and when they did not comprehend, they still mediated with the children by holding them accountable for completing their work.

Parents differed in their approaches to helping their children to succeed academically. Most parents seemed to do well in helping their children on academic activities up to the time they reached the third grade. Before that time, the homework was usually fairly comprehensible for parents who had minimal literacy skills. When children reached the third grade the reading became more complex and some children had moved into all English classes which complicated the issue with homework when they needed help. Parental attention to homework demonstrated the common parent's concern that their children comply with teacher expectations regarding student responsibilities. A few parents worked directly with their children on homework activities by sitting down with them and helping them to interpret their problems and to resolve them. Most parents observed that, for the most part, children were independent about doing their work. In that case, parents helped their children less directly by just monitoring their children's completion of assignments, for example, father checks math problems for Sonia.

Mr. and Mrs. Roble, for example, held Manuel to a consistent routine of doing his homework after dinner. Although he might have been able to do his work independently, Manuel's mother sat with him asking him questions about his assignment and occasionally correcting him.

Mother: ¿Qué es lo que tienes que hacer hoy? *What do you have to do today?*
Manuel: Nomás tengo que hacer estas paginas de cuentas de sumar. *I just have to do these pages of addition problems.*
[Manual's mother sat with him as he worked out his double addition problems and she occasionally asked him to double check his work.]
Mother: No, mira, cuenta otra vez. Aquí tienes que contarle primero y luego sumas lo que sobra con esta linea. *No, look, count again. You have to count this first and carry what is left over with this line.*

[Manual corrected the error and accepted his mother's suggestions to carry the tens place.]

By working with their children at home, parents conveyed the message that school was important and that they wanted to support them to achieve. While parents tried to help their children to complete their homework, many assignments required parents to communicate with the teachers directly in order to clarify an assignment and to better help their children. When this direct contact between parent and teacher occurred, children seemed encouraged to please both the parent and teacher by requesting more homework assignments to improve their work.

On occasion, students did not achieve as quickly as the teacher and the parents expected in spite of the strong support given to them. One example is Lupe Solís who had been doing poorly in her reading and after a few bad reports the mother went to meet with the teacher. Lupe was present at the meeting. Mrs. Solís told the teacher that she had tried to help Lupe with all of the assignments that went home, but the reports still showed that Lupe needed more work. Her mother tried to encourage her by rewarding her for things that she did well every day instead of waiting for the reports at the end of the week. Lupe did not get disillusioned and persisted. Her progress was gradual though slow and she improved her reading to a higher reading level by the end of the year. Again, this illustrated how learning varies for according to their specific zone of proximal development and the importance of having a consistent and systematic mediation by an adult who unconditionally believes in the child (Bronfenbrenner, 1978). Lupe's learning environment was strengthened by the parent's consistent work with her on a daily basis and her achievement in the classroom reflected the parent's work with her in the home.

CONCLUSION

Parents socialize their children to schooling in three major areas—motivation, social adjustment and academic performance. They participate in the rewards and constraints of their children's behavior pertaining to school. This involvement conveys caring, respect, and commitment to their children and for their education.

Parents demonstrated competence in mediating behavioral aspects of their children's educational experiences. Their beliefs and values regarding education were transmitted in discussing school reports and in relating stories about their life in Mexico. By actively mediating in both the school and home settings, the parents assisted children in acquiring acceptable behavior patterns and an identity as a confident learner and problem solver.

The lack of literacy skills in English and the unfamiliarity with the American school curriculum disabled some parents in mediating directly when dealing with specific homework tasks. They were, however, able to mediate their children's studying behavior by monitoring completion of assignments and establishing consistent routines for doing homework. By doing so, children were able to meet their responsibilities at school.

The purpose of parent involvement must be seen beyond the increase in test scores, as important as that may be. Minority families face a complex set of problems in relating to school, especially those from immigrant groups who have not been schooled in this country or groups that have traditionally been marginal. Children's achievement and test scores are but one measure of schooling—social adjustment being another. Furthermore, performance on tests vary at many points of the students' school career. Therefore, the purpose of having mediate their children's learning is to assist them in functioning confidently and independently in their appropriate "zone of proximal development" (Vygotsky, 1978) a concept defined in ecological terms by Bronfenbrenner (1979), thus the insistence of a holistic understanding of the individuals within their social context as described in this chapter between teachers and families. The connections we traced between the individual and the institutional forces that affected them. For this reason, it is crucial that schools make parent involvement an integral part of the curriculum and that functional structures be erected in which parents and teachers can communicate easily and frequently about the children's progress.

The more the parents know about the school the more they can assist their children. In turn, the more teachers know about the child in the home setting, the better they can teach in the classroom. The knowledge which both require to best help children learn is indeed cultural because it is created through interaction in social context. Ultimately parent involvement in their children's education facilitates learning, and that involvement is possible when schools help parents learn about the school's expectations and its operations through a variety of activities. What all of this means on a more macro level is that cultural change on the part of the school *and* the family is necessary to accommodate effective social learning environments for minority children.

REFERENCES

Becher, R.M. (1984). *Parent involvement: A review of research and principles of successful practice.* Washington, DC: National Institute of Education.

Boulder Valley, Colorado, School District. (1975). *A personalized kindergarten program with supplementary parent involvement* (Final Report Submitted to the Bureau of Elementary and Secondary Education). Washington, DC: Office of Education.

Bronfenbrenner. U. (1974a). *A report on longitudinal evaluations of preschool programs. Vol. II: Is early intervention effective?* Washington, DC: Office of Child Development.

Bronfenbrenner, U. (1974b). The origins of alienation. *Scientific American, 231,* 53-61.

Bronfenbrenner, U. (1978). Who needs parent education? *Teachers College Record, 79,* 767-787.

Bronfenbrenner, U. (1979). *The ecology of human development: Experiments by nature and design.* Cambridge, MA: Harvard University Press.

Clark, R.M. (1983). *Family life and school achievement: Why poor black children succeed or fail?* Chicago: University of Chicago Press.

Cole, M., Gay, J., Glick, J.A., & Sharp, D.W. (1971). *The cultural context of learning and thinking.* New York: Basic Books.

Cochran, M., & Henderson, C.R., Jr. (1986). *Family matters: Evaluation of the parental empowerment program.* Unpublished paper. Ithaca, NY: Cornell University.

Comer, J.P. (1984) Home-school relationships as they affect the academic success of children. *Education and Urban Society, 16,* 323-37.

Delgado-Gaitan, C. (1990). *Literacy for empowerment: The role of parents in their children's education.* London: Falmer.

Diaz, S., Moll, L., & Mehan, H. (1986). Sociocultural resources in institution: A context-specific approach. In Bilingual Education Office, Sacramento, CA (Ed.), *Beyond language: Social and cultural factors in schooling language minority students* (pp. 185-228). Los Angeles, CA: Evaluation, Dissemination and Assessment Center, California State University.

Epstein, J.L. (1987). Effects on student achievement of teachers' practices of parental involvement. In S. Silvern (Ed.), *Literacy through family community and school interactions* (pp. 98-110). Greenwich, CT: JAI.

Feuerstein, R. (1980). *Instrumental Enrichment: An intervention program for cognitive modifiability.* Baltimore, MD: University Park Press.

Feuerstein, R., Rand, Y., & Runder, J.E. (1988). *Don't accept me as I am: Helping "retarded" people to excel.* New York: Plenum Press.

Gordon, I. (1978). *What does research say about the effects of parent involvement on schooling?* Paper presented at the Annual Meeting of the Association for Supervision and Curriculum Development. Chicago, IL.

Gotts, E.E. (1980). Long-term effects of a home-oriented preschool program. *Childhood Education, 56,* 228-234.

Gross, M.J., Ridgley, E.M., & Gross, A.E. (1974). *Combined human efforts in evaluating achievement at the Wheatley School*. (ERIC Document Reproduction Service No. ED 102666). Washington, DC.

Herman, J.L., & Yeh, J.P. (1980). *Some effects of parent involvement in schools*. Los Angeles, CA: Center for the Study of Evaluation.

Irvine, D.I. (1979). *Parent involvement affects children's cognitive growth*. Unpublished paper. Albany, NY: University of the State of New York, State Education Department, Division of Research.

Karraker, R.J. (1972). Increasing academic performance through home-managed contingency programs. *The Journal of School Psychology, 10*, 173-179.

Lazar, I., & Darlington, R.B. (1978). *Summary: Lasting effects after preschool* (Monograph Series Paper. Consortium for Longitudinal Studies). New York: Cornell University.

Revicki, D.A. (1981). *The relationship among socioeconomic status, home environment, parent involvement, child self-concept and child achievement*. Unpublished paper. University of North Carolina, Chapel Hill.

Tizard, J., Schofield, W.N., & Hewison, J. (1982). Collaboration between teachers and parents in assisting children's reading. *British Journal of Educational Psychology, 52*, 1-11.

Trueba, H.T. (1989). *Raising silent voices: Educating linguistic minorities for the 21st century*. New York: Newbury House.

United States Census Bureau. (1981). 1980 Census data for Carpinteria, CA.

Vygotsky, L.S. (1978). *Mind in society: The development of higher psychological process* (M. Cole, V. John-Steiner & E. Souberman, trans.). Cambridge, MA: Harvard University Press.

Part III
Schools and Schooling

6
Transition In and Out of the Middle-Level School: The Largest Crack for Disadvantaged Youth

J. Howard Johnston

The tenacity with which humans cling to familiar practices is, at once, one of our most endearing and most frustrating traits. It is the characteristic that gives us comfortable traditions, and it is the one that makes change so difficult. Most important for educators, though, it is the characteristic that makes transition—from home to school, from one school to another, from one grade level to another—deserving of special attention and planning.

Transition difficulties can begin early. As Lightfoot (1978) points out, one of the most difficult transitions occurs between the home and the school. Early on, membership in the school is shown to be based on standards that are quite different from those associated with membership in the family. Discontinuities between the two institutions are produced by both their structural properties and their cultural purposes and, furthermore, these discontinuities are experienced by all children as they move from home to school.

In families, the interactions are functionally diffuse. All of the participants are intimately connected to one another, and membership in the unit is a given. The rights and duties of this membership are all-encompassing, governing even the smallest details of life.

Schools, on the other hand, are functionally specific. That is, relationships are "more circumscribed and defined by the technical competence and individual status of the participants" (Dreeben, 1968). Thus, while attendance is required of all children, full, participating membership in the school group is largely dependent upon performance and competence. More specifically, status and membership, and therefore relationships, are determined by performance and competence *as judged by the teacher.*

Because the schools are public institutions, with allegiance to the public weal and the public order, the nature of relationships between teachers and children reflects "the preparatory, transitional and sorting functions of schools in this society. The roles allocated to children in school are evaluated primarily in terms of their contributions to some future status rather than reflecting full membership in the present society" (Lightfoot, 1978).

Primary schools do, to some degree, replicate the structural properties of the family, rewarding students for some of the same behaviors the family values, such as group maintenance behavior, responsibility and initiative, fundamental "goodness," demonstration of caring, helpfulness, work, and effort. However, the incongruities between school and home become more distinct as the students progress through the system. By later elementary school and early secondary school, few similarities remain between the way one earns status and membership in the middle-level school and the way it is done at home or in the primary grades.

The disruptive nature of this transition from one school to another, and the potential effect on dropout behavior, has long been recognized. As early as 1894, the Committee of Ten on Secondary Studies advocated the restructuring of secondary education, from a 8-4 plan of eight elementary grades and a four-year high school, to a 6-6 or 6-3-3 plan, which was designed, in part, to increase the holding power of the school (National Education Association, 1894). At a time when the dropout rate in the United States approached 75 percent, this committee argued that creating an institutional unit that ended at the 9th grade instead of the 8th could hold students for at least one additional year and perhaps longer.

Implicit in that argument is the knowledge that the point of transition from one school to another—that point at which no social network exists and no sense of institutional membership exists—is a logical point at which to break contact with the institution. The evidence since 1894 has largely confirmed this intuitive sense. It is during the middle grades that a large proportion of dropout-prone youth actually leave school or begin the pattern of absence, truancy, and withdrawal that signals imminent departure from school (Wheelock & Dorman, 1988; Richardson, Casanova, Placiea, & Guilfoyle, 1989).

Early theorists speculated that the transition from the elementary to the middle-level school or from middle to high school was complicated considerably by the stresses that accompany maturation from childhood to adolescence. This orientation led to the view that some amount of tumult was inevitable, and that little could be done except to wait out this developmental storm (Hall, 1904). Since the middle 1960s, however, a view which acknowledges the interactive nature of adolescent development and school practices has prevailed (Eichhorn, 1963, 1966, 1975). More recently, estimates of the number of children experiencing developmental storms and stresses of such a magnitude to interfere with effective schooling have been reduced, and more attention has been focused on actual school practices as predictors of student success, failure, and dropping out (Simmons & Blythe, 1987; Lipsitz, 1984; McDill, 1973; Petersen, 1987).

Among their complex findings, Simmons and Blythe (1987) discovered that multiple transitions—from childhood to puberty coupled with the move from elementary to junior high school—produced adjustment difficulties for students. Multiple transitions seem to have the greatest negative impact on self-esteem. The increased school size of junior high schools, the greater ethnic heterogeneity of the centralized junior high (as distinct from the neighborhood elementary school), and the departmentalization of the secondary school, which requires several peer regroupings during the day, all appear to have an effect on the middle-grades student. While it is difficult to simplify the findings of this large study, there is evidence that these school features are related to diminished self-esteem in both boys and girls and higher rates of victimization (and, therefore, of diminished self-esteem).

Simmons and Blythe conclude:

It was our original hypothesis that this sudden and discontinuous transition from a small, intimate environment to a large, impersonal one would be made more difficult by the large numbers of people and the greater heterogeneity of those people. While these effects are not large, the direction of the effects is generally in line with these hypotheses. We are presuming...that a child suddenly confronted with great numbers of people at a time of a major life course transition will be likely to feel alienated, uncomfortable, and unsure of his or her own self-standing. In this situation, lower self-esteem is likely to result, especially among children lacking in key prior resources and particularly among those who find themselves victimized or held in low regard by these new peers. (1987, p. 340)

The potential effect of declining self-esteem on at-risk students is underscored by the reasons urban youth give for dropping out of school (Fine, 1986). Using ethnographic techniques, Fine identified five clusters of reasons for leaving school:

1. *Perceived low value of a high school diploma.* Lack of evidence in their own experience, often characterized by poverty and chronic family unemployment, that a high school diploma will improve things very much.
2. *Competing responsibilities.* The necessity to contribute to family maintenance or fulfill economic obligations.
3. *Undermined self-esteem.* The incongruity between the traditional, middle-class, authoritarian, adult-controlled environment of the school and their own life experiences are seen as defeating, disenfranchising, and degrading.
4. *School push-out practices and policies.* Practices that actually discourage students from participating in the life of the school and bonding to it and its members.
5. *Pregnancy.* Although it is illegal to expel them, pregnant girls often report feeling so "different" that they cannot remain in the setting.

Implicit in these reasons is a convincing argument that it is necessary to look at educational, social, and economic reasons for school leaving, not just individual developmental patterns. Indeed, lingering just below the surface of these explanations for school withdrawal (and not very far below the surface at that) is the sense that disadvantaged students leave school because they do not "belong" there. Something that the school either does or fails to do interacts with a student's complex history of social, economic, educational, and developmental experiences to invite membership or discourage it. The extent to which that sense of membership is conveyed to the student from the next level of schooling, whether from the middle level or the high school, affects that student's willingness to seek membership in the new setting. Messages of rejection or imminent rejection coming from the school are likely to drive the dropout-vulnerable student into a more comfortable niche—either the familiarity of the streets, or to a job, however menial and low-paying, in which money and self-esteem can be earned.

Gary Wehlage (Wehlage, Rutter, Smith, Lesko, & Fernandez 1989) offers a compelling theory to explain early school leaving on a social membership basis. He argues that students must overcome both *educational impediments* (such as lack of intrinsic and extrinsic rewards for learning school material) and *membership impediments* (such as lack of adjustment to the school context, difficulty with school-managed learning systems, incongruence between school norms and their own experiences, and isolation from the mainstream of school participation) in order to achieve desired school goals. In essence, it is necessary for students to feel that they are *members* of the school, and have a right to that membership, in order for them to succeed there.

Membership, says Wehlage, is based on social bonding, a concept offered by Hirschi (1969) and used, at first, to explain the alienation of delinquent youth. Social bonding has four elements: attachment, commitment, involvement, and belief.

- **Attachment** refers to the social and emotional bonds to others, characterized by whether an individual cares what others think of him and his behavior. It is reciprocal; an individual will not care about others if they believe others do not care about them.
- **Commitment** is the logical part of bonding. It is the belief that remaining connected to a group is the rational thing to do to preserve one's self-interest. Commitment can be based on immediate needs (we stay together for safety) or on long-term, internalized goals (remaining with the group will help me achieve some desired end for myself). In the absence of either a short- or long-term benefit, continued membership in a group is irrational.
- **Involvement** describes the extent of an individual's participation in the activities of the group or institution. For students, this means participation in school activities: academic, social, recreational, and extracurricular. Failing to become engaged, or withdrawing from engagement, often heralds early school leaving.
- **Belief** is faith in the institution or group's legitimacy, efficacy, potency, and continued benefit to the individual. It is a feeling that the group is good for me and that I am good for the group. In short, it determines if a student believes that the school will lead to his or her desired goals.

Clearly, the reasons that Fine gives for urban youth dropping out of school bear remarkable congruence with Hirschi's conceptual framework and Wehlage's argument that the decision to leave is often connected with social rather than developmental or educational issues. Thus, it is equally clear that a student's assessment of the likelihood that he or she will be permitted membership in the institution will affect his or her decision to make an effort to secure that membership. Further, students' perceptions of what awaits them in a school are not only shaped by the experiences that they have already had in other schools, but by the messages sent to them by and about the new institutional environment.

Based on this theoretical framework and conceptual organization, it is essential to uncover what elementary grade students see as impediments to membership in the middle-level school which they are to attend. The concerns and reservations they express during anecdote-telling and other interview formats provide evidence of both the kinds of experiences they have had in school and the kinds of difficulties they anticipate having in the next level of schooling. In essence, it gives insight into both the things they worry about in the school to which they are going and their source of information about the new school.

THE STUDY

Fifty-four fifth- and sixth-grade students about to enter the middle level school were interviewed by the researcher to determine the nature of their concerns about the upcoming transition. The students attended elementary schools in five large cities or transitional suburbs (populations greater than 100,000) throughout the United States. Schools were selected if more than 80 percent of their students were eligible for free lunch; all of the interviewees were free-lunch recipients.

In each school, officials were asked to identify students who fit one of the following two categories:

- *Category I:* Students who had failed one or more grades, but who received no special education services, and who were currently achieving at the 3rd stanine or below on both reading and mathematics achievement tests.
- *Category II:* Students who had never failed a grade, who did not receive any special education services, and who were currently achieving at the 6th stanine or above on both reading and mathematics achievement tests.

For the purposes of this study, Category I students were considered to be at risk of failure and potential dropout behavior in secondary school, Category II students were considered to be at somewhat less risk of failure and dropping out. As a result of this process, 54 children were identified; 30 who were considered to be at-risk, 24 who were not. Table 6.1 shows the demographic characteristics of those students.

Table 6.1.   Demographic Characteristics of Sample

	Students at Risk	Achieving Students
Number	30	24
Ethnicity		
White	17	14
Black	10	7
Hispanic	3	3
Location		
Urban	19	15
Suburban	11	9
Region		
Northeast	9	7
North		
Central	7	7
Southeast	5	4
Northwest	4	3
California	5	3

As an exploratory study, no claims are made that the findings of this investigation are generalizable to the population of at-risk students at large; however, the demographic patterns indicate that the sample itself is largely representative of the urban population of school children in the United States, and of disadvantaged students in particular. Further, the selection criteria employed in this study produced other categorical effects that are worthy of some note.

First, the students in the at-risk category tended to be older than classmates (a function of grade level failure earlier in the elementary years). Almost 90 percent of the members of the at-risk sample were older than their classmates by at least 11 months. In addition, 10 of the students in the at-risk category had an older sibling who had dropped out of school; only two of the students in the achieving group had a sibling who had left school before graduation. Finally, economic status was approximately equal for the two groups. All of the students in the study received free lunches, and all of the students for whom information was available received aid to dependent children appropriate to the county or state in which they resided.

During two one-hour long interviews conducted during the winter and early spring of the 1988–89 school year, the students were queried on a number of issues relevant to school performance, school adjustment, and anticipated performance in the middle-level school. The issues relevant to this chapter are those which deal with the student's anticipated performance and adjustment to the school setting in which they were to be located during the next school year, either a middle school or a junior high school, depending upon the configuration of grades in their school district.

Two forms of queries were used. First, students were asked to describe, as accurately as they could, the school they were to attend the next year. Beyond physical descriptions, they were asked to describe how they thought people were treated in the school (by teachers and students), what a day would be like, and what kind of academic work they thought they would be doing. They were also asked if they knew about extracurricular or other special kinds of school activities and if they planned to participate in them. In each case where the student gave specific information, he or she was asked to identify the source of that information. Second, students were asked to relate a story they had heard about the school and to identify the source of that story.

Three kinds of analysis were undertaken: Student descriptions of the school and its operation were scrutinized for expressions of concern, worry, or anxiety about the forthcoming transition; the sources of information that students relied upon were identified; and student stories were studied to identify the way in which the new school was portrayed in the stories and anecdotes that children were willing to share with the researcher.

The frequency with which groups of students mention certain issues provides a clue to their level of concern about them. The differences between the concerns expressed by at-risk students and the achieving students are striking for their categorical differences. Table 6.2 shows the highly academic nature of the concerns expressed by achieving students and the social-climate issues expressed by at-risk students.

These categories are descriptive of specific concerns expressed by the student interviewees. They may defined as follows:

- *Public Performance:* The performance of an academic task in front of peers. Specific examples included "working problems on the board," "reading aloud to the class," "having to give a speech," or "having your paper read aloud to the class."
- *Mastering Physical Space:* The ability to master the actual physical environment of the new and invariably larger school. Specific concerns included, "getting lost," "not being able to get from one class to another," "not finding places I'm supposed to be," "not being able to work my locker (or other equipment)," or "breaking something."
- *Difficulty of Homework and Tests*: Being overwhelmed by the

Table 6.2.   School Transition Adjustment Issues Identified by At-Risk and Achieving Students (Rank Order of Frequency)

High Achievers	Low Achievers
Public performance (academic)	Grade retention
Mastering physical space	Public performance (academic)
Difficulty of homework and tests	Punishment
Tough standards	Unkind adults
PE: Dressing/shower	Being ridiculed
Failure	Harassment
Grade retention	Difficulty of homework and tests

amount and difficulty of school work. Comments included, "tests every day in math," "a lot of homework every night," "a term paper over the Christmas break," and "having to write compositions every week."

- *Tough Standards*: Having school work and behavior judged and graded very harshly and strictly. Students were concerned about, "teachers just add up the test scores and that's what you get," "they'll give you an F for having the wrong kind of heading on your paper," "Mr. X only gives two A's a year...and only the real smart kids get them," and "they don't let you mess around up there."
- *PE: Dressing/Shower*: Having to participate in a rigorous physical education program that includes judgment of prowess and disrobing for "gang" showers. Comments included, "I don't want to have to take a shower with a big crowd of kids," "they make you keep doing things until you get them right...even if you can't do it," and "I'll probably always be late for my next class after gym."
- *Failure:* Receiving a failing grade on a test or assignment. Students were concerned that, "they give a lot of F's on tests and homework up there," "it's real hard for me to get good grades on homework," and "they make you do things over and over again."
- *Grade Retention:* Being retained or "held back" in a subject or for a whole year. Children expressed concern that "a lot of kids are held back," "if you fail two subjects you have to repeat the whole year," and "I'm afraid I'm going to fail math when it really gets hard."
- *Punishment:* Receiving officially sanctioned school punishments,

such as detentions, suspensions, and others. Students were anxious about "getting detentions for almost nothing," "anyone can put you on detention," and "they suspend you for just about anything there."

- *Unkind adults:* Having to deal with several adults every day, some of whom may be unkind or unpleasant. Students said, "teachers yell a lot there," "they don't help you much...you just have to do it yourself," and "some [teachers, administrators] *try* to get you to break rules so they can nail you."
- *Being ridiculed:* Being teased or demeaned by *other children* for inadequate performance or "doing something stupid." Students said, "other kids really get on you if you screw up," and "I'm always afraid I'll look like a jerk."
- *Harassment:* Being publicly criticized or relentlessly punished by *adults* for no reason the child can understand. They said, "some people just get on you and everything you do is wrong," and "they really get on you at [school]...and they'll do it right in front of the class."

Clearly, the rankings in Table 6.2 show that students who may be considered at-risk are concerned about *the ways in which they will be treated in the school* on a social and school climate dimension. Students who have a history of achievement are concerned, primarily, with the *academic challenges of the new school.* In short, at-risk students worry that they will not be treated fairly as human beings...as members of the school community. Achieving students are worried about their ability to fulfill the expectations of the institution, not as members, but as performers of the institutions publicly stated goals and objectives.

None of these children, however, had ever experienced the school to which they are going. How can they have such specific reservations? In order to address that question, students were asked, "Where did you hear about [a specific concern the student mentioned]?" They were also asked, "If you wanted information about the new school, where would you get it?"

Somewhat surprisingly, both at-risk and achieving students tend to rely upon the same sources of information about their new school, and each group depends equally upon each source. Table 6.3 gives the rank-ordering of information sources about the new school for each group. These ranks were determined by the frequency with which each source was mentioned voluntarily during the interviews ("My brother told me it's really neat up there.") and in response to the questions noted above.

Table 6.3.   Sources of Information About the New School (Rank Order)

At-Risk Group	Achieving Group
Teachers in Present School	Teachers in Present School
Friends/Siblings Attending New School	Friends Attending Present School
Friends Attending Present School	Friends/Siblings Attending New School
Parents, Other Relatives	Parents, Other Relatives
Official School Information	Official School Information

Clearly, students utilize information resources that are outside of the official communication prepared by the receiving school. Teachers, seen as system insiders if not directly "inside" the new school, have considerable credibility. Thus, the messages they send to students have a relatively profound influence on the views of the receiving school formed by its potential students. Beyond that source, students tend to rely on siblings and peers, then adult family members, and, finally, official school communications (such as orientation programs, printed materials, introductory visits from middle-level school personnel to their elementary schools). One student went so far as to say, "You really can't believe much that the [middle school] tells you. Even the kids they send down here to talk to us are all the teachers' favorites...the real good kids. They just tell us what the school wants us to hear."

DISCUSSION

At-risk students differ from achieving students in the concerns they have about moving into the middle-level school. Most significantly, at-risk students are concerned about very fundamental matters: whether they will fail and be retained, whether they will be subjected to arbitrary punishments by unkind adults, and whether they will be ridiculed and harassed by students and adults alike. They are the concerns expressed by people who are uncomfortable with the very idea of being *present* in a given setting. The fears and apprehensions are about conditions which are unrelated in any significant way to their academic performance, but to simply being tolerated, not punished for being there.

It is also significant that the information about what awaits them at the middle-level school comes from the same sources as students who are relatively comfortable with their sense of belonging. Achieving students have few doubts that they will be at least *tolerated*; most feel that they will actually be welcomed. This means that the same sources are giving very different messages to these groups of students. Teachers are, evidently, communicating one scenario to at-risk students and another to achieving students.

Even peers and siblings carry different messages. Because school grouping practices make it unlikely that at-risk students will have significant associations with achieving students (Oakes, 1985), the information coming back to at-risk students from the new school is likely to come from their friends and siblings...people who hold many of the same beliefs and values. Achieving students, on the other hand, evidently get messages which indicate that their membership is, at least, assured; it is only their academic performance that will result in negative judgments by authorities in the new school.

The findings from this series of interviews is consistent with the membership theory advanced by Wehlage and his colleagues (1989). At-risk students are apprehensive about the social treatment they will receive at the hands of the receiving school. Academic issues become a concern only to the extent that they affect their sense of belonging in the institution (fear of public criticism, grade retention, etc.). In short, at-risk students have concerns for their social psychological safety.

Perhaps most important, the sources of information about the new school can be viewed from their respective memberships as well. Teachers are clearly perceived as members of the school organization. Therefore, they are likely to be good sources of information, even if the information they give to at-risk students is somewhat frightening ("You won't get away with that kind of sloppy work up *there*."). So, although at-risk students may not be able to readily identify with teachers on a personal basis, it is clear that they are a good source of information about schools.

By the same token, people with whom the at-risk student *can* identify on a personal basis will also be considered credible sources of information about the new school if they have firsthand experience with it. Indeed, the message that older peers and siblings already enrolled in the school may convey is that "people like *us* aren't welcome here." If the at-risk student sees himself as a reasonable replication of the person giving the information, it is easy then for him to expect the same kind of treatment being given to his information source, either his peer or his sibling.

This suggests that both the content of the messages being given to students *and* the nature of the messengers may have to change if at-risk students' apprehensions about entering middle-level schools are to be reduced. If schools seek to engage their students, as Wehlage suggests, not only in the educative processes of the school but as full-fledged members as well, specific and careful attention needs to be given to the early perceptions of the institution formed by incoming youth.

REFERENCES

Dreeben, R. (1968). *On what is learned in school.* Reading, MA: Addison-Wesley.

Eichhorn, D.H. (1963). Biological correlates of behavior. In H. W. Stevenson (Ed.), *Child psychology, sixty second yearbook of the NSSE* (Part I, pp. 16-33). Chicago: University of Chicago Press.

Eichhorn, D.H. (1966). *The middle school.* New York: Center for Applied Research. (Reprinted, 1987, Reston, VA: National Association of Secondary School Principals)

Eichhorn, D.H. (1975). Asynchronizations in adolescent development. In S.E. Dragastin & G.H. Elder (Eds.), *Adolescence and the life cycle* (pp. 161-201). New York: Halstead.

Fine, M. (1986, Spring). Why urban adolescents drop out of high school. *Teachers College Record, 87,*(3), 393-409.

Hall, G. S. (1904). *Adolescence: Its psychology and its relations to physiology, anthropology, sociology, sex, crime, religion and education* (Vol. I and II). New York: D. Appleton.

Hirschi, T. (1969). *Causes of delinquency.* Los Angeles: University of California Press.

Lightfoot, S.L. (1978). *Worlds apart.* Cambridge, MA: Harvard University Press.

Lipsitz, J. (1984). *Successful schools for young adolescents.* New Brunswick, NJ: Transaction Books.

McDill, E.L., & Rigsby, L.C. (1973). *Structure and process in secondary schools: The academic impact of educational climates.* Baltimore: Johns Hopkins University Press.

National Education Association. (1894) *Report of the committee of ten on secondary studies.* New York: American Book Company.

Oakes, J. (1985). *Keeping track.* New Haven, CT: Yale University Press.

Petersen, A.C. (1987, September). Those gangly years. *Psychology Today, 21,* 28-34.

Richardson, V., Casanova, U., Placier, P., & Guilfoyle, K. (1989). *School children at risk.* New York: Falmer Press.

Simmons, R.G., & Blythe, D.A. (1987). *Moving into adolescence: The impact of pubertal change and school context*. New York: Aldine De Gruyter.

Wehlage, G.G., Rutter, R.A., Smith, G.A., Lesko, N., & Fernandez, R.R. (1989). *Reducing the risk: Schools as communities of support*. New York: Falmer Press.

Wheelock, A., & Dorman, G. (1988). *Before it's too late*. Boston: Massachusetts Advocacy Center.

7

Teachers' Conceptions of Ability: Implications for Low-Status Students

Roger L. Collins

SOCIAL COMPARISON AND LOW ACHIEVING STUDENTS

It is not at all surprising that researchers have discovered that low achieving students are often disadvantaged by comparisons with their higher achieving classmates. Levine (1983), for example, reports that social comparisons of low-achieving students with their higher-achieving peers are likely to produce feelings of inferiority, reduced motivation, and hostility among low-achieving students. On the other hand, the higher status accorded higher-achieving students is associated with more opportunities to perform in the classroom and more interpersonal influence among students, even when the achievement that is the basis for their higher status is not related to the task at hand (Berger & Fisek, 1974).

In the late 1970s Steve Bossert (1979), among others (e.g., Marshall, 1976), identified specific features of classroom organization that served to either accentuate or deemphasize the amount of social comparison that took place in classrooms. He identified classrooms that accentuated interpersonal comparisons among students as "high resolution" classrooms and those that reduced comparisons as "low resolution" classrooms. Bossert differentiated four aspects of classroom organization that contribute to the amount of social comparison among students: (a) the degree to which the teacher and students are responsible for selecting academic tasks; (b) the degree to which the teacher and students are responsible for determining the nature, structure, or procedures of the academic tasks; (c) within-classroom grouping practices; and (d) academic performance evaluation practices.

In high-resolution classrooms, task selection, task structure, grouping, and evaluation practices serve to accentuate social comparisons among students. With respect to task selection and task structure, high-resolution classrooms are characterized by the teacher's selection of learning goals, the creation and direction of learning tasks, sequence and pace of learning tasks, and the social context in which tasks are undertaken. Bossert observed that classrooms organized in this manner resulted in less variation across learning tasks which made it easier for students to engage in comparisons among their performances. Similarly, whole classroom instruction or the creation of clearly defined ability groups facilitate comparisons among students' performances. The use of ability groups within classrooms can further facilitate comparisons among students in those classrooms where there are different learning tasks and treatment of students according to ability group placement. Finally, classroom performance evaluations that are very public, frequent, comparative, and related to only a few skill domains facilitate comparisons among students.

In contrast, low-resolution classrooms are characterized by greater autonomy in students' choices about what school work to do and how and when to do it. The greater number of different performances initiated by students reduces the ease and standardization of comparisons among students. In low-resolution classrooms, students work individually or in small groups varyingly composed. Students work together in small groups because of similar interests, or to address specific and short-term skill needs, or to promote interaction among students from different backgrounds. The variety of bases for grouping students makes it more difficult for students to assign comparative meaning to students' placements in small groups. Finally, in low-resolution classrooms, students' performance evaluations are less public, less frequent, and are related to more performance areas than in high-resolution classrooms.

Although Bossert (1979) described relationships between classroom structure and social comparisons among students along four dimensions of classroom organization, others have since noted the complexity of interacting aspects of classroom organization within the across these four dimensions (Marshall & Weinstein, 1984). These authors note that several aspects of classroom organization might contribute to the ease of social comparison while other aspects do not. For example, with respect to performance evaluations, a given classroom might publicly display students' achievements in a wide variety of performance domains. Despite the public nature of the evaluations, the diversity of performance domains reduces easy comparisons among students. There are contextual factors that influence the ease with which students can engage in social comparison as a result of the teacher's use of ability grouping. For example, the relative amount of student mobility across such groups would influence the ease or difficulty of social comparisons. The teacher's procedures in the conduct of small group work might also contribute to the ease or difficulty of social comparisons. It would seem easier, for example, for students to make comparisons in classrooms where students can observe the teacher working with one small group at a time than in classrooms where students are engaged in tasks as the teacher circulates.

It would appear, therefore, that the relative ease or difficulty of students' engagement in social comparison is determined by a variety of interacting aspects of classroom structure. The dimensions identified by Bossert (1979) and the differentiations of these noted by Marshall and Weinstein (1984) provide useful directions for analyzing relationships between classroom structure and students' social behaviors. Such analyses have revealed that certain classroom structures may be more problematic for low-achieving students than others.

One particular series of studies has indicated that classrooms characterized as facilitating students' social comparisons are more likely to have a higher proportion of students identify themselves as low-ability students than classrooms that reduce social comparison among students (Rosenholtz & Simpson, 1984; Simpson, 1981). In addition, classrooms characterized as more socially comparative have a higher rate of agreement among students and between students and their teachers regarding the ability hierarchy among the students in those classrooms (Rosenholtz & Wilson, 1980; Rosenholtz, 1982; Simpson, 1981). In classrooms where "low achievers" are so readily and consensually identified, the problems associated with that identity are more likely to occur. These problems include feelings of inferiority attributed to low ability; attributions more likely to depress students' motivation to persist on learning tasks than attributions of insufficient effort or inappropriate task difficulty (Rosenholtz & Simpson, 1984).

There is some evidence from the research literature that the hierarchical position of low-status students in high-resolution classrooms can be improved by expanding the repertoire of academic performances that are elicited and rewarded in the classroom. Susan Rosenholtz (1977, 1979, 1984) refers to this expanded repertoire of academic performances as the "multiple abilities" curriculum. The basic premise of her intervention is that both the advantages of high status and the disadvantages of low status can be reduced by increasing the variety of performance domains in the classroom (Rosenholtz, 1984, p. 458). Her assumption is that students will demonstrate different levels of performance in accordance with the different abilities elicited by a "multiple abilities" curriculum.

The specific abilities elicited by her particular intervention included visual thinking, intuitive thinking, and reasoning. In her experiments visual thinking was defined as forming and manipulating visual images in problem-solving tasks. Intuitive thinking was defined as making inferences based on limited information. Reasoning was defined as deductive thinking and inductive thinking. Her general observations of teaching lead her to conclude that visual and intuitive thinking were abilities that were not often utilized in traditional classrooms. Further, her assumption was that the hierarchy of student performances in these two additional aspects of ability would vary from the established hierarchy based on a more narrow conception of ability.

The results of her intervention appear to support her assumptions. While sharp differences in interpersonal influence between high- and low-status students persisted in the control group classrooms, high- and low-status students occupied high and low influence ranks with equal probability in the multiple ability classrooms (Rosenholtz, 1984, p. 461). Further, the multiple abilities curriculum intervention appeared to have elevated the performance expectations of low-status students and reduced the difference in high- and low-status students' self-evaluations. Students in the multiple abilities classroom appear to have engaged in differential self-evaluations: 58 percent gave self-ratings that were not the same on each of the three abilities that comprised the curriculum. In conclusion, Rosenholtz offers that the multiple abilities curriculum provides multiple bases for status within the classroom and for self-evaluation. She also criticizes well-intentioned emphasis on "the basics" in the classroom: "the teacher who emphasizes back to basics in order to raise the performance level of previous low achievers...narrows the definition of legitimate academic performance thus stratifying performance expectations in the classroom with the ironic outcome that previous low performers are likely to consolidate their low self-concepts" (Rosenholtz & Simpson, 1984, p. 57).

COGNITIVE ORIGINS OF CLASSROOM STRUCTURE: TEACHERS' CONCEPTIONS OF ABILITY

Previous research on instructional innovation and planned efforts to change teachers' instructional behavior indicates that teachers' ability and willingness to change depend, in part, on the correspondence between the theories that underlie their current teaching and the theories that underlie the innovation (Fenstermacher, 1979, 1987; Floden, 1985; Glaser, Abelson, & Garrison, 1983). Several investigators of classroom structure (e.g., Marshall & Weinstein, 1984, p. 321; Rosenholtz & Simpson, 1984, p. 40) presume that the primary origin of a classroom's high or low resolution lies in the classroom teacher's conception of ability. These authors reason that teachers who view ability as a general and stable trait that crystallizes relatively early in a person's development are more likely to generate high-resolution learning environments.

The notion that an individual's ability is general and stable has also been referred to as a fixed or "entity" view of ability (Dweck & Elliot, 1983). This conception of ability is reflected in the assumption that there is a high correspondence between students' performances among various and diverse subject areas (e.g., Boersma, Chapman, & Macguire, 1979) or the assumption that performance in reading, for example, is highly correlated with performance on tasks unrelated to reading skill (e.g., Tammivaara, 1982). The notion that ability is relatively stable is reflected in many students' and teachers' assumptions that students' early grades in school are predictive of later grades (e.g., Bloom 1976; Entwisle & Hayduk, 1978). Interestingly, the more extreme assumption that intelligence is fixed at birth and changes little with age is held by only a small minority of Americans (Brim, Glass, Neulinger, & Firestone, 1969).

Taken together, these particular conceptions of ability provide a foundation for the construction of learning environments that (a) identify a relatively narrow range of skills, primarily verbal, that are viewed as central to school performance; (b) position the teacher as exclusively responsible for maintaining student attention to those skill areas; (c) view students along a stable ability hierarchy with concomitantly differential expectations and treatments; and (d) evaluate and publicize student performances along this range of skills in a socially comparative fashion. Of course, this theoretical delineation of relationships between a particular conception of ability and the construction of a corresponding learning environment uses the extreme case in order to illustrate the theoretical premise. It is likely that teachers' conceptions of ability are more moderate than depicted here and perhaps, even inconsistent. The point of this exercise, however, is to demonstrate the potential ways in which a particular conception of ability might be connected to the learning environment created by the person holding that view.

A parallel theoretical delineation of the conceptual foundations of the low-resolution classroom can also be constructed. In contrast to the entity view of ability, an "incremental" view assumes that an individual's ability is composed of a repertoire of skills that are independent and continually transformed by experience (Dweck & Elliot, 1983). The theory that intelligence is best characterized as a set of independent "intelligences" has been most recently reflected in the work of Howard Gardner (1985). The notion that intellectual capacity can be enhanced by experience is a relatively popular view of intelligence (Brim, Glass, Neulinger, & Firestone, 1969, p. 20) and one that is receiving increasing theoretical and empirical support (Feuerstein, 1979, 1980).

An incremental conception of ability is a more likely conceptual foundation for the low resolution classroom than the entity view of ability. The multitask (Bossert, 1979), multidimensional (Rosenholtz & Simpson, 1984) learning environments that characterize the low-resolution classroom would seem to be preferred by teachers who acknowledge and seek to engage and challenge a variety of abilities within and among students. The teacher's acceptance of divergence among students' performances would appear to be grounded in a conception of ability that is multifaceted (Marshall & Weinstein, 1984, p. 307). The acceptability of a multiplicity of skills within and among students is a basis for encouraging students to exercise greater control over the selection of content, sequence, and pace of learning activities. The teacher may be less inclined to focus students' attention on a predetermined set of skills and more likely to permit students to pursue self-determined directions in their pursuit of learning.

With respect to grouping students in the classroom, a teacher holding an incremental view of ability, which assumes students possess multiple abilities, is less likely to support the idea of ability grouping when the criterion for grouping is narrowly defined. In cases where ability grouping is school policy, one might assume that those teachers holding an incremental view of ability would be more likely to promote a higher rate of mobility across ability groups. Also, one would assume that teachers holding an incremental view would make use of a variety of abilities, interests, and other characteristics of students as bases for forming groups in the classroom. Finally, the incremental view of ability would more likely avoid an absolute standard for evaluating students' school performance and, instead, encourage evaluation in a variety of performance areas. Whether such multiple evaluations were relatively public or private, one would assume that they would be less socially comparative than in the high resolution classroom. When considered as a cohesive conceptual framework, albeit a theoretically posited framework, the incremental view of ability would appear to provide a conceptual foundation for the low resolution classroom.

Although it would be inappropriate to hold the low resolution classroom as a universally ideal model, the socioemotional benefits of such classrooms, for low achievers especially, would indicate that features of the low-resolution classroom should be among the learning environments teachers can choose to implement. As indicated earlier, however, teachers' readiness to implement one or more of these features may depend on the conception of ability they hold. From the perspective of teacher preparation, it is important to consider the range of conceptions of ability prospective teachers bring to the context of teacher preparation and to consider the ways in which teacher preparation contributes to those conceptions of ability.

THE FORMATION OF CONCEPTIONS OF ABILITY: IMPLICATIONS FOR TEACHER PREPARATION

There has been some controversy over the question of the origins and the evolution of individuals' conceptions of ability. It had been widely assumed that individuals develop a conception of ability that progresses from an incremental view toward an entity view of ability (Dweck & Elliot, 1983, p. 675; Nicholls, 1978). The assumption had been that during their school years children develop a mature view of ability as a more global and stable characteristic. Other researchers, however, have questioned this assumption on theoretical and empirical grounds. A competing explanation for differences among individuals' conceptions of ability has been the social constructionist view that assumes that conceptions of ability are based on the institutionalized conceptions of ability that surround the individual (Berger & Luckman, 1966; Rosenholtz & Simpson, 1984).

There is some evidence, for example, that students hold relative entity or incremental views of ability in accordance with the relative high or low resolution of their respective classrooms (Rosenholtz & Simpson, 1984). Those high-resolution learning environments that define learning tasks and implement student grouping and performance evaluations in ways that "construct" ability as a global and stable entity are more likely to promote entity views of ability among students than low resolution classrooms. The significant differences in views of ability that exist among children and adults, including college students (e.g., Surber, 1984), within a given culture and between cultures (e.g., Holloway, 1989; Wober, 1974) suggest that views of ability are acquired through socializing experiences in schools and at home. The social constructionist perspective raises questions concerning how the socializing experiences of teacher preparation interact with the conceptions of ability students bring with them. To what extent do experiences in teacher preparation contribute to particular conceptions of ability held by prospective teachers?

Responses to this question can only be speculative at this time. There has been no research regarding the perspectives teacher trainees bring to their teacher preparation experiences and no research on the influence of those experiences on prospective teachers' conceptions of ability. Speculation might begin, however, with a consideration of the degree to which teacher preparation explicitly acknowledges and examines the social constructionist perspective. One might argue that the social constructionist perspective provides a tool for analyzing various aspects of teaching, learning, and knowledge as socially constructed. This epistemological framework provides a context for construing ability as socially constructed. There has been concern, however, that teacher education has come to underemphasize the socially constructed nature of schooling in general (Beyer & Zeichner, 1987). The concern of these critics of teacher education has been that current emphasis on an "objectivist" conception of knowledge and schooling has overemphasized teaching as a specific set of skills and competencies apart from the social contexts and social goals of the enterprise.

These authors have argued that attention to the "technical" competencies of teaching is not necessarily problematic but does reflect a misplaced emphasis given the range of social, moral, and ethical dilemmas that confront the existing practices of schooling. Their concern has been that human engineering approaches to teacher preparation accept existing institutional definitions of constructs that need to be reexamined (Popkewitz, Tabachnick, & Zeichner, 1979). Teacher education that emphasizes "survival training" and the integration of its graduates into the current social structures of schooling is seen as less likely to encourage prospective teachers to deal critically with that reality in order to improve it (Beyer & Zeichner, 1987, p. 312). Teacher education within this perspective would tend to avoid the social and political consequences of how ability is defined. The emphasis instead would be on how to improve students' abilities, however defined.

The issues raised previously regarding teacher education can also be considered more generally with respect to the college curriculum. At this more general level the question becomes: To what extent does the college curriculum define knowledge as given or as problematical (Ginsburg, 1986)? To what extent does the curriculum view knowledge as "truth, out there" or as tentatively constructed and subject to political, cultural, and social influences? Bernstein (1972) referred to these contrasting views as "traditional" and "progressive" respectively. Again, it would seem that more "progressive" perspectives would create contexts in which prospective teachers would be able to construe knowledge, including concepts of ability, as socially constructed. These teachers, therefore, are more likely to see a role for themselves and others in the social construction of ability within their classrooms.

Another aspect of institutional socialization that may influence prospective teachers' conceptions of ability is the manner in which their institutions define ability with regard to their performance. This aspect of institutional socialization begins with seeking admission to the college. Does the institution operationalize singular or multiple conceptions of ability in defining criteria for admissions? The same question can be raised with respect to admissions to departmental programs, performance evaluations in class, and criteria for successful program completion. It is interesting to note that colleges seeking recognition as elite institutions often attempt to support their claims of selectivity by reducing yet dramatizing their institutionalized indicators of ability (Kamens, 1977). If this tendency applied to all colleges of education with aspirations of achieving higher status and recognition, one inadvertent consequence could be the socializing of prospective teachers toward a more narrow conception of ability.

CONCLUSION

There is substantial evidence that students' comparisons of their school performances is harmful to low-achieving students when comparisons are made within the narrowly defined performance domains of the "traditional" classroom. Low-achieving students are more likely to improve their self-evaluations and self-expectations in learning environments that provide multiple performance domains in which they can define themselves as competent students. Improved self-esteem and self-expectations provide a foundation for persistence on a variety of school tasks, including those that challenge students. The emotional risks entailed in confronting one's own challenges in the classroom are reduced by the sense of efficacy established in other, less personally challenging performance domains. The improved social status of the heretofore low-achieving students also serves as a basis for increased participation in academically productive social relations with classmates.

Opportunities for students to participate in learning environments that provide multiple domains for their performances, self-definitions, and peer evaluations may depend on the conception of ability held by teachers and teachers' knowledge of classroom activities and structures that actualize that conception of ability. Whether teacher education programs can provide the learning and socializing contexts that contribute to thinking about ability as multifaceted and incremental remains a question. One question raised by many teacher educators has been the degrees to which teacher education transforms and/or reproduces social inequalities. This question has usually been posed in conceptual/theoretical or ideological terms: What theories, concepts, and ideologies underlie the teacher education curriculum, the social relations between students and faculty and among faculty, and the institutional relations between teacher education programs and the schools that assist in teacher preparation? Further, how do these theories, concepts, and ideologies interact with those held by teacher trainees?

With respect to the present theme concerning classroom organization and its consequences for low-achieving students, similar questions can be raised. To what extent does the faculty possess and actualize multifaceted and incremental concepts of ability in their relations with students and each other? To what extent are these views connected to theories and practices of teaching in the curriculum? What are the varying impacts of these views on the implicit theories held by teacher trainees and how can these interactions of views provide opportunities for learning? To what extent are these views acceptable to the administrators, cooperating teachers, parents, and students in the schools where student teachers practice their profession? All of these questions remain to be answered but there is ample evidence that they need to be posed by practitioners and researchers.

REFERENCES

Berger, J., & Fisek, M.H. (1974). A generalization of the status characteristics and expectation states theory. In J. Berger, T.L. Conner, & M.H. Fisek (Eds.), *Expectation states theory: A theoretical research program.* Cambridge, MA: Winthrop.

Berger, P., & Luckman, T. (1966). *The social construction of reality.* Garden City, NY: Doubleday & Co.

Bernstein, B. (1972). On classification and framing of educational knowledge. In M. Young (Ed.), *Knowledge and control.* London: Collier-Macmillan.

Beyer, L., & Zeichner, K. (1987). Teacher education in cultural context: Beyond reproduction. In T. Popkewitz (Ed.), *Critical studies in teacher education.* London: Falmer Press.

Bloom, B.S. (1976). *Human characteristics and school learning.* New York: McGraw-Hill.

Boersma, F.J., Chapman, J.W., & Macguire, T.O. (1979). The student perception of ability scale: An instrument for measuring academic self-concept in elementary school children. *Educational and Psychological Measurement, 39,* 135-141.

Bossert, S.T. (1979). *Tasks and social relationships in classrooms.* Cambridge: Cambridge University Press.

Brim, O., Glass, D., Neulinger, J., & Firestone, I. (1969). *American beliefs and attitudes about intelligence.* New York: Russell Sage Foundation.

Dweck, C.S., & Elliot, E.S. (1983). Achievement motivation. In P. Mussen & M. Hetherington (Eds.), *Handbook of child psychology, Vol. IV: Socialization, personality, & social development.* New York: John Wiley.

Entwisle, D., & Hayduk, L. (1978). *Too great expectations: The academic outlook of young children.* Baltimore: John Hopkins University Press.

Fenstermacher, G. (1979). A philosophical consideration of recent research on teacher effectiveness. In L.S Shulman (Ed.), *Review of research in education,* (Vol. 6). Itasca, IL: F.E. Peacock.

Fenstermacher, G. (1987). On understanding the connections between classroom research and teacher change. *Theory into Practice, 26*(1), 3-7.

Feuerstein, R. (1979). *The dynamic assessment of retarded performers.* Baltimore: University Park Press.

Feuerstein, R. (1980). *Instrumental enrichment.* Baltimore: University Park Press.

Floden, R. (1985). The role of rhetoric in changing teachers' beliefs. *Teaching and Teacher Education, 1*(1), 19-32.

Gardner, H. (1985). *Frames of mind: The theory of multiple intelligences.* New York: Basic Books.

Ginsburg, M. (1986). Reproduction, contradictions, and conceptions of curriculum in preservice teacher education. *Curriculum Inquiry, 16*(3), 283-309.

Glaser, E., Abelson, H., & Garrison, K. (1983). *Putting knowledge to use.* San Francisco: Jossey Bass.

Holloway, S.D. (1989). Concepts of ability and effort in Japan and the United States. *Review of Educational Research, 58*(3), 327-345.

Kamens, D. (1977). Legitimating myths and educational organization: The relationship between organizational ideology and formal structure. *American Sociological Review, 42,* 208-219.

Levine, J.M. (1983). Social comparisons and education. In J.M. Levine & W.C. Wang (Eds.), *Teacher and student perceptions: Implications for learning.* Hillsdale, NJ: Erlbaum.

Marshall, H.H. (1976). *Dimensions of classroom structure and functioning project: Final report.* Berkeley, CA: University of California.

Marshall, H.H., & Weinstein, R.S. (1984). Classroom factors affecting students' self-evaluations: An interaction model. *Review of Educational Research, 54*(3), 301-325.

Nicholls, J.G. (1978). The development of concepts of effort and ability, perception of own attainment, and the understanding that difficult tasks require more ability. *Child development, 49*, 800-814.

Popkewitz, T., Tabachnick, B.R., & Zeichner, K. (1979). Dulling the senses: Research in teacher education. *Journal of Teacher Education, 30*(5), 52-60.

Rosenholtz, S.J. (1977). *The multiple abilities curriculum: An intervention against the self-fulfilling prophecy.* Unpublished doctoral dissertation, Stanford University, Stanford, CA.

Rosenholtz, S.J. (1979). The classroom equalizer. *Teacher, 97*, 78-79.

Rosenholtz, S.J. (1982). Organizational determinants of classroom power. *Journal of Experimental Education, 50*, 83-87.

Rosenholtz, S.J. (1984). Modifying status expectations in the traditional classroom. In J. Berger & M. Zelditch (Eds.), *Status, rewards, and influence.* San Francisco: Jossey Bass.

Rosenholtz, S.J., & Simpson, C. (1984). The formation of ability conceptions: Developmental trend or social comparison? *Review of Educational Research, 54*(1), 31-63.

Rosenholtz, S.J., & Wilson, B. (1980). The effect of classroom structure on shared perceptions of ability. *American Educational Research Journal, 17*, 75-82.

Simpson, C. (1981). Classroom structure and the organization of ability. *Sociology of Education, 54*, 120-132.

Surber, C.F. (1984). The development of achievement related judgment processes. In J.G. Nicholls (Ed.), *Advances in motivation and achievement* (Vol. 3). Greenwich, CT: JAI Press.

Tammivaara, J.S. (1982). The effects of task structure on beliefs about competence and participation in small groups. *Sociology of Education, 55*, 212-222.

Wober, M. (1974). Towards an understanding of the Kiganda concept of intelligence. In J. Berry & P.R. Dasen (Eds.), *Culture and cognition: Readings in cross-cultural psychology.* London: Methuen & Co. Ltd.

8
Friendly Text: A Bridge to Children's Literacy Learning

Johanna S. DeStefano

Growing poverty in the inner cities, hypersegregation reported in 10 major metropolitan areas, alarming dropout rates, widespread literacy problems reported in national studies—how are they all connected? For one, reading "failure,"—whatever that may be—is often asserted to be at the heart of school failure which, in turn, leads to more dropouts, which in its turn has been correlated with more poverty. Correlation does not signal cause and effect; certain scholars such as Harvey Graff (1987) argue that greater literacy levels and upward mobility are not even correlated, let alone causally related. However, those who have experience in inner-city schools in our large cities are well aware that these characteristics often cluster within certain minority groups such as African-Americans, Hispanics, and Appalachians.

According to Mikulecky (1987), the 1989 National Assessment of Educational Progress (NAEP) data show that "on the average, Black and Hispanic 17-year-olds read approximately as well as the average White 13-year-old." Further, dropout rates in many urban schools, where the economically disadvantaged often cluster, are at 50 percent or more, while in some states such as Minnesota and Wisconsin, nearly two-thirds of the 18-year-olds go to college. He notes that "an urban Black or Hispanic student has nearly the same likelihood of dropping out of high school as a non-urban White has of enrolling in college" (1987, p. 17).

The two economically disadvantaged groups of particular interest to me are the urban African-American and the urban Appalachian.

The latter, although white, nonetheless constitutes a substantial portion of economically disadvantaged, at-risk children in many urban schools such as those in Cincinnati and Columbus, OH. These two groups are both subordinated cultures in the United States, although they have very different origins. Ogbu (1988) describes African-Americans as a castelike or subordinated minority group, relegated to menial positions in the society and denied real assimilation into mainstream culture. Even though Appalachians have an early settlement history in the United States and are white, they too have subordinated cultural characteristics, though perhaps not a castelike position such as African-Americans and Native Americans.

Out of these subordinated cultures arise secondary cultural and language differences from the mainstream majority. Ogbu (1988) suggests they develop these differences of behavior and attitudes to protect their collective and social identity and to maintain boundaries between themselves and others. Certainly both groups may use varieties of American English which are "marked" for ethnicity and class. Many urban African-Americans speak Black English or Black Vernacular, while many Appalachians typically speak South Midland dialect, frequently called Appalachian English. (See Wolfram & Christian, 1976, for a description of this variety.)

Strong correlations have been formed among lower levels of literacy, high dropout rates, and the use of socially stigmatized varieties of American English, such as Black English and Appalachian English. Smitherman (1981) notes that African-American males are overrepresented among school dropouts, the incarcerated, the unemployed, and among those speaking Black English. The literacy level in Appalachia where the widely stigmatized dialect of South Midland is spoken is, for example, critically low when compared with that of other areas in the United States (Wolfram & Christian, 1978).

This profile does not appear to be that different for urban Appalachians, who constitute an "invisible" yet substantial minority group in at least 30 major eastern, northern, midwestern and southern cities (McCoy, Brown, & Watkins, 1981). In some cases, such as in Atlanta, Appalachians' actual numbers are greater than the numbers of African-American migrants from the rural South. In fact, more than 3,000,000 migrants from the Appalachian region settled in cities such as Chicago, Cincinnati, Columbus, Washington, D.C., Tampa/St. Petersburg, and even Los Angeles during the 20-year period following World War II. This trend has continued despite a brief period of return migration to rural and mining settlements during the early 1980s.

When literacy becomes part of an equation which apparently yields the vicious cycle indicated above, that variable brings in language, as literacy is itself a language activity learned and used in contexts in which oral language is also used. Here is the conundrum. It's relatively safe to say that virtually all children, by the time they come to school, have very good control over the oral language forms which are part of their cultures and speech communities, that is, those which are appropriate for and experienced by young children. This language ability or communicative competence (DeStefano, 1978) as it's often called, is a major strength that the disadvantaged child brings to school, and a significant portion of it is in the form of ability to engage in dialogue.

For those of us who are educators and deeply concerned with the disadvantaged student, a major question is how can this language strength the children already have be used as a bridge to literacy? If they are literate, they are not likely to persist with *that* problem and perhaps with other difficulties such as underemployment, unemployment, school failure based on inability to read and write, in addition to the rest of the characteristics which round out the profile of a growing underclass in the United States.

THE TOM, DICK, AND HARRY DIALOGUE STUDIES

Based on my interest, as a sociolinguist, in the intersection among oral language use both at home and school, sociocultural group or speech community membership, and written texts used for literacy instruction, colleagues and I conducted two studies, which I call the Tom, Dick and Harry dialogue studies. The major purpose of the studies was to shed some light on the higher rates of illiteracy among two at-risk groups, urban African-Americans and urban Appalachians, through an analysis of discourse in various contexts, both spoken and written. In the first study (DeStefano, Pepinsky, & Sanders, 1982; DeStefano, 1984) I was particularly interested in connections between how each of three boys, one each from Appalachian, African-American, and mainstream groups, interacted orally with their first-grade teacher during literacy learning sessions using basal readers as the primary vehicle for literacy instruction, and how each was learning to read. For this study, among other analytic formats, I used cohesion analysis to analyze their dialogue with the teacher. The particular form of cohesion analysis is the one described by Halliday and Hasan in their 1976 volume, *Cohesion in English.*

The second, later study (DeStefano & Kantor, 1988) was conducted in three homes, using the dialogue produced by a mother–child dyad from each of the same three groups in the original study. This study also included an analysis of dialogue in two types of early reading materials: stories from first-grade, primer-level basal readers, and children's storybooks written by authors and usually read to children. The first study prompted this second study, especially the analysis of written dialogue in these materials. Cohesion analysis again was used, but with some modifications to incorporate Halliday's and Halliday and Hasan's later work (Halliday, 1985; Halliday & Hasan, 1980), which includes an analysis of tie chains.

These two studies allowed me to analyze four basic dialogue groups: mother–child, teacher–student, characters in primer-level basal reader stories, and characters in children's storybooks read to children in the early years. I compared and contrasted not only within these dialogue groups but also across the groups, when I had comparable data.

One may well ask why all these comparisons, and why the selection of dialogue for such comparisons. When one considers that reading may well be "an unnatural act," both ontogenetically and phylogenetically, one begins to think about what might be bridges from children's producing and comprehending the spoken language to their learning to read written text. It seems relatively evident that dialogue is the major form of input for children, the language matrix of daily interaction from getting up in the morning to going to bed at night, including television. The ubiquitousness of dialogue cuts across sociocultural groups in the United States and is probably a language development universal. People talk, adults talk with children, children talk with adults, and children talk with children. If dialogue then is a dominant oral language form and the one with which children probably have the most experience, it stands to reason that the use of dialogue may serve as a bridge to literacy learning.

Perhaps we could think of oral dialogue as "friendly text," especially if we take Dreher and Singer's definition as "one [a text] that has features that facilitate learning from it" (1989, p. 98). It's clear that children, as they develop oral language, learn not only language but also about people and the world around them via interaction with other speaker/listeners in interactive, dialogic situations. Perhaps dialogue is maximally friendly text; here I use Halliday's definition of text as "any passage, spoken or written, of whatever length, that does form a unified whole" (Halliday & Hasan, 1976, p. 1), as it includes oral language as well as written. At any rate, dialogue is ubiquitous, useful, and controlled by virtually all children. Here then is a major oral language base upon which to construct a bridge to literacy, and possibly the clearest bridge from oral to written modes.

In an attempt to gain some understanding of "bridge building" or a lack thereof, we looked at initial literacy materials, especially the prevalent basal primer, and selected children's storybooks. Based on their research, Freebody and Baker (1985) state why we did emphasize basals: "They [basal readers] are written to help teach young children (in the first 2 to 3 years of school) how to read; and they are, more broadly, stepping-stones from oral, conversational conventions of communication to those which apply in a written, literate context" (1985, p. 381). They go on to note that "much of what children first read at school *is* in the form of written reportage of oral talk" (Baker & Freebody, 1986, p. 452). Evidently these initial literacy materials are supposed to provide for the necessary transition from comprehending oral dialogue to comprehending written dialogue. That's why we chose to investigate them.

Not only are they supposed to provide a transition, but basals also are used for initial literacy instruction in around 85–90 percent of first-grade classrooms in the United States. Since their use is so widespread, their impact on economically disadvantaged children must be understood better than it currently is. For example, Pappas and Brown (1989, p. 111) ask a very important question which we are still struggling to answer: "What will children learn from reading passages from a basal like the following?":

    Bob
    Bob likes to fish.
    Why?
    Why does Bob like to fish?

    Bob likes to fish.
    That is why
    he likes to fish.
        (Smith & Wardhaugh, 1980, pp. 49–50)

Can such a story provide for the transition from comprehension of oral dialogue to written dialogue? Does its strangeness have a connection with why so many children are not making a bridge from oral language to written language, from spoken dialogue to written dialogue found in abundance in these early literacy materials? Might written dialogue, admittedly with many different forms from the oral as written language constitutes a different set of registers, somehow be "unfriendly" text? If so, how? And might a teacher's behavior be able to modify a text's apparent "unfriendliness," as Dreher and Singer (1989) suggest?

In order to being to answer the above questions, in the Tom, Dick, and Harry dialogue studies we looked at one characteristic of dialogue, both oral and written. The oral dialogue we selected involved boys and their mothers and boys and their first-grade teacher. The written form was found in basals and children's storybooks, the latter of which are more "user-friendly" as texts, not having the shorter sentences and constrained vocabulary of the basals. This language characteristic has been called cohesion by Halliday and Hasan in their seminal book, *Cohesion in English* (1976). It is important, in part, because it's an aspect of both spoken and written language, a type of language universal. Thus an analysis of cohesion allows us to compare and contrast across registers, modes, and other distinctions which differentiate among uses to which language may be put.

While cohesion analysis is an important analytical tool for linguists and sociolinguists such as myself, it also makes important connections to the processes involved in being literate. Hence its ultimate usefulness in our continuing struggle to better understand the plight of economically disadvantaged children from the standpoint of concern about the much higher levels of illiteracy for that group. More detail on cohesion analysis will be presented below.

READING COMPREHENSION AND COHESION

A major piece of the puzzle lies in our understanding or lack of understanding of reading. Reading by itself is an essential part of literacy in American society and is a complicated process of comprehension. It is a receptive process that "starts," perhaps trivially, with the graphic display as input and ends with meaning as output, to use a computer metaphor. The reader arrives at meaning via cycles of sampling, predicting, testing, confirming (Smith, 1978), and integrating (Pearson & Spiro, 1980), relying on strategies (Beck, 1985; Wilson & Anderson, 1985) which yield the most reliable prediction. Thus, in reading, information from the text and the knowledge possessed by the reader act together to produce meaning (Schallert, 1982) in a dynamic process.

Much of the research effort into comprehension is now focused on how readers comprehend a variety of passages. Central to this effort is the understanding that written text includes chains that create a coherent set of ideas, *and* the ability of the reader to follow those cohesive chains of ties, to be able to "preserve the links" (Chapman, 1989). We are now beginning to appreciate the complexity of processing necessary for recognizing text coherence, since the unity is often implicit rather than explicit (Chapman, 1979; Fredericksen, 1977; Irwin, 1983). Children's difficulties arising from this complex processing of coherence seem dependent in large measure on the amount of tacit information that must be "known" to make the text comprehensible (Chapman, 1987; Irwin, 1986).

Unfortunately this issue of implicit versus explicit cohesion has been generally neglected in early reading. As a result, the child may well be faced with establishing cohesion in the absence of many of the most useful and common cues that permit cohesion if they are not included in the beginning reading materials (Chapman, 1983; Rutter & Raban, 1982). This process may be extremely difficult for those economically disadvantaged children who may not be experienced with literacy, although all children are "preliterate." These "school-dependent children" may need more support from schooling itself to provide some of what we know other children often experience at home.

How much do they know when they approach the task of learning to read? Literacy research (e.g., Chapman, 1981; Irwin, 1986) indicates that a reader applies his or her knowledge of cohesion when he or she interacts with a text. It is held that if there is a continuity between the reader's cohesion strategies and those in the text, the reader will be able to supply the missing pieces and the components necessary in the total picture in order to "approximate" the writer's intention, for example, follow an argument (Chapman, 1989; Irwin, 1983; Kintsch & Vipond, 1978; Marshall & Glock, 1978).

What are the links from cohesion in text to comprehension in reading? We certainly don't know them in enough detail, but research (Irwin, 1980; Marshall & Glock, 1978) indicate that these links are far from tenuous. Chapman (1987, p. 26) concisely describes a part of the linkage.

> Presupposition in the sense used here can be related to recent thinking in the study of reading because it goes a long way to explain the process of prediction or anticipation that comprises a large part of the reading process. In essence readers on perceiving the onset of a cohesive tie know, not only from the content (which is related to the top-down factor of the reading process we mentioned earlier), but from their knowledge of the language, that the other end of the tie will inevitably follow. This is regardless of the distance in terms of words, sentences or even paragraphs that separated the beginning and end of the tie. It is proposed therefore that the ability of readers to tie the tie, or effect tie closure, is an important concomitant of reading fluency.

It should be noted that Chapman's use of the term "fluency" does not imply ability to read aloud well. It's a British term akin to our American notion of ability to read with comprehension, without laboring.

Coherence is the missing ingredient in Chapman's analysis of the relationship between textual coherence and reading comprehension. Chapman asserts "The cohesive ties are shown to be assembled in chains that run through the text providing chains of identity and similarity, and, according to latest proposals, establish coherence" (1984, p. 9). Hasan (1984, p. 1) states that "cohesion is the phenomenon on which the foundation of coherence is laid..." Cohesion via *substitution* may be at the noun or nominal level as in "*car parts*...the *ones*," at the verb level as in "*feed* their young with milk...animals which *do this*...," and at the clause level itself as in "Do you think you'll be able to come tomorrow? I hope *so*." *So* is a substitute for "I'll be able to come tomorrow." A fourth type of cohesive tie is *ellipsis* in which a word or phrase represents a whole segment which appeared before it. An example is "What color did Jim paint the dog house?" "Red." in which the answer "red" stands for "Jim painted the dog house red." Much may be left out in the answer because the information is presupposed in the question itself. The final type of cohesive tie is *conjunction*, a very complex category due to the possible types found in English. For example, a conjunction may be adversative as in "She said that he wasn't supposed to be there. *But* he appeared anyway."

Halliday and Hasan (1980; Halliday, 1985) later proposed the notion of chains, formed by a series a cohesive ties related in different ways, which may "run" throughout the text. They propose two major types of chains: *identity* and *similarity*. The semantic bonds underlying these two types are distinctly different. Identity ties, when one lexical item refers to another, form an identity chain and have their shared reference, or co-referentiality, as their semantic bond. For example, identity chains are formed through pronominal usage (Tom = he), generic lexical repetition (girl = girl), and ellipsis ["I am going to school. Are you?" (going to school)]. These chains introduce both the speakers and the topics spoken about in dialogue and cohere these two elements throughout the text. So a speaker thread begins and is woven into the text, as well as topics being introduced and maintained throughout a piece of dialogue.

One could simplistically diagram in a linear fashion the relationship of the three elements—cohesion, coherence, and comprehension:

cohesion	*coherence*	*comprehension*
in text →	in text →	in reader of text
	and reader	

The concept of cohesion will be presented in greater detail below. Coherence has also been described by Moe and Irwin (1986) as a "cognitive correlate of cohesion," implying that it is primarily for the reader to establish and is not embedded in the text. Others, notably Hasan (1984), have argued that textual elements, including cohesion, help establish coherence *within* the text. I suspect coherence—whatever it is—is achieved by a process of the reader interacting with aspects of the text. Comprehension is now frequently considered to be a largely reader-based process, rather than text-based, as a more dynamic, interactional model of reading has gained support.

Chapman (1989) indicated some parameters of the link between cohesion and comprehension when he concluded from his massive research study of middle school readers in the UK (reported in Chapman, 1987), that a reader needs to be able to preserve the links in text (cohesive ties and chains) and process those links as well. He noted that poor readers, who don't comprehend well, seem to get lost in cohesive chains and have trouble maintaining the thread of meaning in chains. He concludes that "cohesive tie anticipation and chain monitoring [are] integral parts of the reading process" (1987, p. 93).

Whatever comprehension may be is not as important in this discussion as the realization that learning to read, to become literate in some sense, necessarily and crucially involves comprehension. Simply, where there is no comprehension, there is also no reading. As Chapman (1984, p. 9) puts it so well, "growth in reading [is] a process in which students are learning how to mean within the textual function of language." A major part of "textual function" is cohesion, or rather the cohesive devices available in a language which provide much of the semantic linkage in a text via various lexical choices.

TEXTUAL COHESION

Why cohesion has this evident role in comprehension is better understood when one knows more about the concept. Halliday and Hasan (1976) describe textual cohesion as an integrative property that provides text with its semantic unity. The linkages which establish cohesion are called *ties*, and a single instance of cohesion ties: lexical, reference, substitution, ellipsis and conjunction, as well as two major types of chains—identity and similarity (Halliday & Hasan, 1980; Hasan, 1979).

Lexical ties are important cohesive devices in that they establish much of the "content" of text. Reiteration is one basic type which may be accomplished through a repetition of the same word, through use of a synonymous set such as *help* and *aid*, by use of antonyms, by use of a superordinate term such as *flower* linked to a subordinate term like *nasturtium*, and by use of a whole-part relationship such as *care* and *tire*. Cohesion via reiteration in its various forms is an important part of creating similarity chains in text (more about these below).

Reference cohesion is frequently achieved through the use of various kinds of pronouns, common ones being like *she* of "*Margie...she...*"

Similarity ties—when one lexical unit relates in meaning to another to form a similarity chain—have coclassification (classified in the same semantic category) or coextension (meaning relations within the same semantic field) as their semantic bond. Lexical reiteration (girl/girl, look/glance), antonomy (good/bad), hyponomy (flower/rose), and meronomy (table/leg) are examples of co-extension. As Hasan (Halliday & Hasan, 1980, p. 51) puts it, "Each such chain is made up of items which refer to non-identical members of the same class of things, events, and so forth, or to members of non-identical but realted classes of things, events. etc." In a sense, the elaboration and development of the topics introduced is accomplished via similarity chaining, so we find not identity but relatedness and *extension* of meaning already established.

This very brief sketch of types of cohesive ties does not do justice to the system, but for purposes of discussion of the data in the Tom, Dick, and Harry studies, it will suffice. (For much greater detail, see Halliday & Hasan, 1976, and Chapman, 1983.)

According to Chapman (1989), readers must "track" the chains and ties in a text in order to comprehend it. So we are back to the research questions. Why do some children, who are adept at oral dialogue comprehension and production, seem not to be able to make the transfer to comprehending written dialogue? And what role might cohesion play in understanding this dilemma? These were the questions, among others, which motivated the two studies described below.

TEXT IN SCHOOL: TOM, DICK AND HARRY IN FIRST GRADE

In the first study (DeStefano et al., 1982; DeStefano, 1984, 1991), my colleagues and I focused on the dialogue between a first grade teacher and our child participants—Tom, an Appalachian boy, Dick, an African-American boy, and Harry, a mainstream boy. We also focused on their "success" in becoming literate, as measured in a variety of ways. (See DeStefano et al., 1982, for a description of these measures plus the study's procedures.)

Within the 1976 framework of cohesion analysis which was available at the time, we first analyzed the dialogue for types of cohesive ties which we hypothesized might show relatedness in the dialogue between the teacher and the boys, building toward shared meaning within which to learn literacy. I also looked at the teacher's part of the dialogue itself, as it was so dominant in the text sampled. Later we asked questions about building shared meaning by mothers and their three-year-olds, Tom, Dick and Harry "revisited" as young children.

In the data I found a phenomenon I called tie domination which indicates relatedness and "sharing" in dialogue. To determine the direction of domination of ties, for example, teacher-dominated or student-dominated, I made four separate determinations:

1. teacher ties with self (with her own discourse)
2. teacher ties with student
3. student ties with teacher
4. student ties with self, with his own discourse.

Numbers 1 and 3 are teacher-dominated in that the first cohesive item in a tie set is selected by the teacher. Numbers 2 and 4 are student-dominated for the same reason.

I found around 42 percent of all ties present in the dialogue analyzed were made by the teacher back to items she had selected. Further, 28.5 percent of all the ties in the discourse were made by the students to items in the teacher's speech. Thus slightly over 70 percent of all ties produced were dominated by the teacher, either by tying with her own speech or by students' tying to her speech. There was relatedness in the dialogue, but little "negotiated" meaning as the topics were teacher introduced and lead.

The other 30 percent of all ties found in the dialogue were student-dominated, but largely because they initiated a tie by asking for help with reading. Thus the teacher's tie response was to answer a student question. This pattern suggests a dependency relationship for the boys since the teacher set the task which prompted the questions.

Predominating types of cohesion produced by the teacher and by Tom, Dick, and Harry were also determined. The three major types of cohesive devices found in the data were lexical, ellipsis, and reference, with virtually no use of either substitution or conjunction. Within these categories, only a few cohesive possibilities were utilized by the interactants, demonstrating little of the cohesive variety possible in English. Also, differential patterns of cohesion use were found in the teacher's speech and in that of Tom, Dick, and Harry's. She almost exclusively used certain types of reference and lexical reiteration to achieve what cohesion there was in her discourse. Even more narrowly, most of the teacher's lexical cohesion was achieved through the repetition of items, so that she accomplished cohesion through the use of the same item with an identical reference, only one of the ways to achieve lexical cohesions. Her discourse was replete with:

Is that *Bill*?
Yes, it does look like *Bill*.
Where does it look like *Bill's* going?

The teacher's portion of classroom instructional dialogue sounded like an oral version of "primerese," the stereotyped language of the first-grade basal readers.

When the students' cohesive devices were analyzed, we found that while many of the devices employed by Tom, Dick, and Harry in their reading groups were different from the teacher's, some were the same, and yet all converged toward the linguistic demands of her discourse. Further, there were no major differences among the boys in the types of cohesive devices employed in their speech, no matter what their ethnolinguistic group membership.

What could we make of these findings in conjunctions with the boys' reading profiles? In the case of Tom, the urban Appalachian child, and Dick, the urban African-American child, it is clear that their initial experiences with literacy in the first years of schooling were judged by the teacher to be less successful than those of Harry, the mainstream boy. It was also clear that Tom did not read as well as Harry, while Dick's ability was somewhere between the two. In terms of attitudes or "insights" about reading, the three boys all expressed the opinion that kids would do better in first grade if they already knew how to read when they came to school. (The boys' reading levels are described in greater detail in DeStefano et al., 1982.)

We found, then, that successful oral discourse learning or dialogue display did not seem to clearly connect with the boys' imputed success in literacy learning. In other words, we found "business as usual" in this classroom, with the mainstream boy, Harry, being judged more successful in literacy learning than either Tom or Dick, both from "at-risk" groups. This conclusion led to even more questions about the connection between oral dialogue and written dialogue, and about how educators could build on the first to help "at-risk" children more successfully learn the second. Since I didn't find many clues to help answer these questions in this first study, another colleague and I (DeStefano & Kantor, 1988) turned to the home, specifically to Tom, Dick, and Harry as three-year-olds learning oral dialogue with their mothers. We hoped to make a clearer determination of possible bridges to literacy which could be used by educators. We also included an analysis of written dialogue for the reasons I discussed previously.

TEXT AT HOME: TOM, DICK, AND HARRY AS PRESCHOOLERS

Mother–child interactive language was chosen as the exemplar of informal dialogue because of its apparent importance in the language development process. However, there may be speech community and sociocultural group differences in the forms such interaction take. For example, it has been shown (Blount, 1972; Ferguson, 1977) that mainstream culture mothers, whether consciously or unconsciously, appear to act and speak in ways which facilitate their children's language use patterns viewed as acceptable by the schools. Within the African-American sociocultural group, it's clear that some language interaction patterns between adults and children differ from those in middle-class culture (Taylor & Dorsey-Gaines, 1988; Ward, 1971). Comparable data are virtually nonexistent for Appalachian homes. However, within that group there are attitudes toward language behavior expressed in folk sayings such as "Talk is women's work." Further it is reported that boys are often socialized not to talk much. An urban Appalachian cultural informant notes that a companionable silence is highly regarded by men, which can often stretch into 10 to 15 minutes at a time, or longer (cf. Hansel et al., 1990).

Even with the paucity of data, it is nonetheless clear that mothers in both these groups use language to socialize their children to the language use patterns typical of each. Wells (1986) reports from his Bristol, England, study that in all cases, parents' talk was more diverse and "enabling" of learning than teachers' talk. This finding held across the families representing all income groups. We had no reason to think that this was not the case in our sample. But the lack of information on mother–child interaction in these two major sociocultural groups in the United States made the need to collect data on those dialogue patterns even more compelling, especially as we had no other cohesion analyses for these groups.

We conducted primary, direct observation of dialogue between a mother and her three-year-old preschool son in homes of the same three sociocultural groups as in the previous study—another Tom, Dick, and Harry, if you will. Each set of texts of mother–child dialogue was then subjected to an expanded cohesion analysis which included the analysis of chains not found in the 1976 version (Halliday, 1985; Halliday & Hasan, 1976, 1980). Selection of the dyads, and data collection and analysis procedures are reported in DeStefano and Kantor (1988).

WRITTERN TEXT: DIALOGUE IN BASAL READERS AND CHILDREN'S STORYBOOKS

A sample of dialogue from commercial basal readers and a sample of dialogue from preschool-level children's literature stories were chosen as exemplars of the written discourse children are exposed to early in literacy instruction. Primers, the beginning books in basal reading series, tend to be characterized by short, choppy sentences and repetitive vocabulary selected for the sake of so-called "readability" (Anderson, 1982), plus a lack of aspects of "storiness" (Bettelheim & Zelan, 1981; Steinberg & Bruce, 1980). (Remember why Jim likes to fish. It's because he likes to fish! But I don't think this is offered as an epistimological issue.)

The basal reader stories were chosen from among commonly used series in a major midwestern city's public school system where the three-year-olds' brothers were in first grade, another "comparability check" with the original Tom, Dick, and Harry. The three commercial series sampled were Ginn (Clymer & Venezky, 1982); Holt, Rinehart and Winston (Everetts, Weiss, & Cruickshank, n.d.-a, n.d.-b); and Houghton-Mifflin (Davis, n.d.; Durr et al., n.d.), with two stories from each for a total of six primer stories. Six basal stories had to be used in order to provide an amount of dialogue comparable to the three children's literature stories. The dialogue, both spoken and written, was then subjected to cohesion analysis (Halliday, 1985; Halliday & Hasan, 1976, 1980).

We also sampled from selected children's storybooks, which are typically written in a more coherent style than basal primer stories, yet obviously different from spoken discourse. The written dialogue was sampled from *Mr. Rabbit and the Lovely Present* (Zolotow, 1962); *The Grouchy Ladybug* (Carle, 1977); and *Harry and the Terrible Whatzit* (Gackenback, 1984). These are all storybooks which our sample would have read to them by teachers during their pre-first-grade experience. These stories form a part of the written discourse most children are exposed to, and they are also considered by educators to be part of the bridge to literacy discussed above.

COHESION IN SPOKEN AND WRITTEN DIALOGUE

Unlike the first study, the data were largely analyzed for identity and similarity chains across both spoken and written text and across the three ethnolinguistic groups. We found various cohesive ties forming into identity chains. The clearest result was the frequent use of ellipsis, at around a similar level (25% to 36%) in the dialogue of the three dyads and the children's storybooks. (Remember that ellipsis was Tom, Dick, and Harry's most predominating tie form in their dialogue in the first-grade study.) However, ellipsis represented only 4 percent of all tie types in basal stories.

In basals, the distribution of the other tie types was divided between pronominal usage and exact repetition. Generic repetition

(59%) as in *truck-truck-truck* or *trade-trade-trade*, was the main mechanism of identity chain topic tying in basal stories, with pronominals, the second most prevalent cohesive device, occurring as 37 percent of all tie types. This heavy use of repetition is much involved in producing what is termed "basalese" or "primerese."

In the first study, the teacher's main tie type was generic repetition, the same as in the basal samples. Her second major type was pronominal reference, again like the basals. She could be characterized as producing an oral version of "primerese," at least in terms of cohesive ties. In comparison, in the children's storybook dialogue, generic repetition as a tie type was only 18 percent of all ties, the lowest level in all categories of ties across oral and written dialogue. The predominant tie type was pronominalization at 46 percent of all ties. The use of both pronominalization and ellipsis was much closer to the mother–child dialogue patterns of topic ties forming identity chains.

In a general sense, similarity in cohesion is an indication of how, once the meaning is established through identity chains, it develops and expands. We found that the three sociocultural groups produced similar numbers of similarity chains (19.5, 15.3, and 20), in spite of widely differing text lengths measured in number of utterances and tokens. (For greater detail on all these areas, see DeStefano & Kantor, 1988.)

Children's stories had considerably more similarity chains than the basal stories. This was in contrast to their equal number of identity chains and despite their much longer length than the basals. Thus, the basal and children's stories introduced and maintained the same amount of information via identity cohesion, but differed radically in the development and expansion of that information through similarity cohesive devices. This stands to reason as basal stories are constrained by their relatively short text length, although there is no inherent reason why they should be so short.

Within spoken dialogue, all three sociocultural groups were more similar than different in their production of cohesive chains. The three dyads differed most in terms of text length and the establishment of identity, and differed less in terms of similarity development. Their differences could be characterized more as quantitative (amount of text and amount of topic information), while their similarities could be characterized more as qualitative (how they developed the topic information).

Within written dialogue, storybooks and basal readers shared only one text cohesion characteristic: The same amount of topic information was introduced in each genre through an identical number of topic identity chains. The differences in their text characteristics were many. Storybooks were twice as long as basals. Basals had the greatest amount of repetition across all categories of identity tie types in either mode, spoken or written, while storybooks had the least amount of repetition. Basals used almost no ellipsis, while children's storybooks used a great deal, and storybooks had far more similarity chains and similarity ties than basals. Finally, the pattern of usage of similarity tie types was relatively even across all categories of ties for storybooks, while basals relied mostly on lexical reiteration to achieve similarity chaining. Basal stories and children's literature stories were both quantitatively *and* qualitatively different, except for the amount of information introduced via identity chains.

Across modes, there were many cohesion features in common between storybooks and the spoken mother–child dialogue sampled. Storybooks and all three mother–child dyads shared similar patterns of usage in identity tie types and similarity tie types. On the other hand, the teacher's part of the dialogue was most similar to the basal tie types. Thus the "school dialogue" experience, both oral and written, was different from home talk and from children's literature, both of which children are obviously the most exposed to before they come to school.

DISCUSSION

Given the major impetus of these studies, namely to try to better understand how language use, sociocultural group or speech community membership, literacy materials, and literacy learning sessions interact to contribute to the disproportionate literacy failure among urban Appalachian and African-American children, what insights might we have gained from the above findings and procedures? If we can accept the importance of dialogue as a bridge from comprehending oral to comprehending written text, and I think there are good reasons why we can, some of the studies' findings are helpful in understanding this above interaction. However, it is clear that we are dealing with complex factors interacting in a complex manner collaborating to produce an all too clear result—disproportionate literacy failure among economically disadvantaged children. These factors, which were not researched in the two studies my colleagues and I conducted, include: peer group language interaction and attitudes toward language use, sociocultural group/subordinated culture conflict with and hostility toward the school, and little to no adaptation of materials and methods used in classrooms to be more culturally responsive to these children, or even awareness of their own literacy resources or possible bridges to literacy.

Thinking about what might constitute friendly or unfriendly text for disadvantaged children, we found that cohesion analysis of the spoken dialogue in both studies revealed more similarities than differences, except for the teacher's speech. For example, it was clear that the mother–child dyads were more similar than different in their use of cohesion, as were Tom, Dick, and Harry in the first study. So oral dialogue would seem to constitute "friendly" text in which the children competently participated across speech communities. And so did the dialogue in children's storybooks, which was more similar to oral dialogue than not, on the basis of cohesion. As we have been able to link cohesion to coherence to comprehension, I would argue that aspects of cohesion are an important component in determining the friendliness of a text, thus a possible better match in initial literacy instruction. Cohesion can also demonstrate important similarities or differences among language users.

The analysis procedure also revealed that the cohesion patterns in the children's and mother's dialogue and in the written dialogue of children's storybooks were both qualitatively and quantitatively different from the patterns found in the sampled basal reader stories and in the first-grade teacher's speech. In terms of the cohesion types and their distribution in the data, neither the mother–child spoken discourse nor the written discourse found in the children's storybooks matched that of the basals or the teacher's. Basal dialogue, whether spoken or written, is truly in a class by itself, at least in these samples from the Ginn, Houghton Mifflin, and Holt Rinehart and Winston first-grade readers, and from our teacher in reading groups in which she was using an earlier Holt, Rinehart and Winston basal series than the one sampled in the second study. In fact, Gourley (1984) calls such dialogue deviant.

A major reason basal stories seem so anomalous is that they tend to rely on very few forms of cohesion possible in English and also used in other forms of dialogue. Irwin (1986) reports the same sort of finding in her survey of research on basal stories. When lexical reiteration achieved by generic repetion of the same item—*truck-truck-truck*—is the overwhelmingly dominant form of cohesion used, several problems crop up. They are, to quote Irwin (1986, p. 64), (a) a reduction in…"natural redundancy in which the use of different words provides [at least] two ways of viewing the same topic, and (b) it results in the imprecise use of the reiterated words, resulting in lack of clarity." These problems are also problems of comprehension, a major goal of reading instruction.

These comprehension problems the cohesion analysis revealed are based on the lack of similarity chains in primer stories in relation to the number of identity chains. Identity chains introduce the speakers and topics, while similarity chains develop and elaborate on that information. We found children's storybooks had considerably more similarity chains than did basal stories. This is in contrast to their equal number of identity chains and despite their major differences in story length. In other words, there weren't more chains just because the stories were longer. Thus, both basals and children's stories introduce and maintain the same amount of information via identity cohesion, but differ radically in the development and elaboration of that information via similarity cohesive devices. The basal story requires, in a sense, much more comprehension as a reader has greater detail to fill in and more inferring to do, based on less information about connections, less redundancy, elaborated meaning, and so on. A primer story is almost a kind of shorthand, with a great deal of information packed into a small space. I think it's safe to say that for some children, such text is extremely unfriendly. It seems to be more so for economically disadvantaged children, although it is not the only reason for such disproportionate literacy failure on their part.

Shouldn't we think instead of using the oral language experiences and knowledge Toms and Dicks in particular bring to school with them as a bridge to reading other sorts of books more closely resembling spoken cohesion patterns which are communicative in intent? On the basis of cohesion analysis, this would clearly imply a larger role for children's storybooks in initial reading instruction. It also suggests other kinds of books. Baker and Freebody argue from their textbook analysis "that early reading books could be written to more closely represent children's conversational practices and problems as naturalistic research has shown them to be..." (1986, p. 481).

While I agree there could be rewriting of basal text to render it more friendly, I also would like to argue that the data suggest the use of already existing, friendly written text (in terms of similarity of cohesive devices), namely children's storybooks. Such a movement is already underway in a variety of classrooms but could be much more extensive than it is, especially with economically disadvantaged children who often experience fewer educational "winds of change" and less research-based practice. Their own stories also can be used to form a bridge to literacy, their own language dictated to and written by someone in the classroom. Both these text types constitute more friendly text than do basal primer stories.

Another schooling strategy suggested by the research is implied in the contrast between the mothers' use of cohesion and the teacher's. Obviously we have a limited sample, but it still affords us a glimpse of processes warranting thought and future research. The teacher's cohesion devices, when teaching reading, were as limited as those of the basal stories. Thus, what the stories didn't supply to establish coherence and comprehension, Tom, Dick, and Harry did not get from her mediation of the written text. If anything, her speech only served as a reinforcement of the same devices which, if they weren't helpful in establishing coherence, more of the same wouldn't be either. Thus teachers need to be sure to do more of what mothers and characters in children's storybooks do—conduct more elaborated, exploratory dialogue using similarity chaining which fosters important intellectual development via the use of synonyms, antonyms and so on. Wells (1986) noted that all the parents he sampled provided more stimulating talk than the teachers. Further, expanded use of cohesive devices could possibly render basal text less unfriendly.

These studies have presented us with an interesting conundrum, however, as our Toms and Dicks were not very different from our Harrys or their mothers when we analyzed their dialogue. Yet the first-grade study showed Harry to be doing somewhat better in learning to read, apart from the teacher's perception. Cohesion analysis as it was done in these studies does not reveal why this is the case. The explanation may lie in mainstream culture children's capacity to "ignore" basals, understanding that primers don't have much to do with literacy, that they do *not* provide the transition from oral dialogue to written dialogue. If a child doesn't try to understand primer stories, perhaps he or she is better off. (Remember why Jim likes to fish!) Treating them as opportunities for word recognition practice may be what many better readers do. Perhaps economically disadvantaged children, some of whom have limited literacy experiences, actually view them as *stories*, not as exercises. Somehow these primers have a differential impact on children in urban Appalachian and African-American speech communities. This should not surprise us. As early as 65 B.C., Lucretius pointed out, "What is food to one man may be fierce poison to others" (656 B.C. [?], 637). Further research will have to sort out why basals are meat to some and "fierce poison" to others.

In closing, I caution us to be mindful that literacy is at base a language activity. Thus is it important not to forget to approach literacy learning with this in mind, armed with a better understanding of what could be called the "glue" of language—cohesion.

REFERENCES

Anderson, R. (1982, April 16). *Comments in Staff Summary, Hearing on Language and Literacy*. U. S. Department of Education, National Commission on Excellence in Education, Houston, TX.

Baker, C.D., & Freebody, P. (1986). Representations of questioning and answering in children's first school books. *Language in Society, 15*, 451-484.

Beck, I. (1985). Five problems with children's comprehension in the primary grades. In J. Osborn, P.T. Wilson, & R.C. Anderson (Eds.), *Reading education: Foundations for a literate America* (pp. 239-253). Lexington, MA: Lexington Books.

Bettelheim, B., & Zelan, K. (1981). Why children don't like to read. *The Atlantic Monthly, 248*, 25-31.

Blount, B. (1972). Parental speech and language acquisition: Some Luo and Samoan examples. *Anthropological Linguistics, 14*, 119-130.

Carle, E. (1977). *The grouchy ladybug*. New York: Crowell Junior Books.

Chapman, L.J. (1979). The perception of language cohesion during fluent reading. In P.A. Kolers, M.E. Wrolstad, & H. Bouma (Eds.), *Processing of visible language I*. New York: Plenum.

Chapman, L.J. (1981). *The comprehension of anaphora*. An ERIC document—ED205897.

Chapman, L.J. (1983). *Reading development and cohesion*. London: Heinemann Educational Books Ltd.

Chapman, L.J. (1984). *Cohesion and reading comprehension*. Paper presented to the World Congress of Applied Linguistics, Brussels, Belgium.

Chapman, L.J. (1987). *Reading: From 5-11 years*. Milton Keynes, England: Open University Press.

Chapman, L.J. (1989). Readability Special Interest Group presentation, International Reading Association convention, New Orleans, LA.

Clymer, T. & Venezky, R. (Eds.). (1982). The trade Ken made (no author). In *Inside my hat* (pp. 51-57, first-grade basal reader). Lexington, MA: Ginn & Co.

Davis, J. (n.d.). Too little, too big. In W. Durr, J. LePere, J. Pikulski, & M.L. Alsin (Eds.), *Boats* (pp. 46-54, first-grade basal reader). Boston: Houghton Mifflin.

DeStefano, J.S. (1978). *Language, the learner and the school*. New York: John Wiley & Sons.

DeStefano, J.S. (1984). Learning to communicate in the classroom. In A.D. Pellegrini & T.D. Yawkey (Eds.), *The development of oral and written language* (pp. 155-165). Norwood, NJ: Ablex.

DeStefano, J.S. (1991). Ethnolinguistic minority groups and literacy: Tom, Dick, and Harry at home and in school. In M. McGroarty & C. Faltis (Eds.), *Languages in school and society: policy and pedagogy*.

DeStefano, J.S., & Kantor, R. (1988). Cohesion in spoken and written dialogue: An investigation of cultural and textual constraints. *Linguistics and Education, 1*(2), 105-124.

DeStefano, J.S., Pepinsky, H.B., & Sanders, T.S. (1982). Discourse rules for literacy learning in a classroom. In L. Cherry-Wilkinson (Ed.), *Communicating in the classroom* (pp. 101-129). New York: Academic Press.

Dreher, M.J., & Singer, H. (1989). Friendly texts and text-friendly teachers. *Theory Into Practice, XXVIII*(2), 98-104.

Durr, W., LePere, J., Pikulski, J., & Alsin, M.L. (Eds.). (n.d.). A fish for Sam. In *Balloons* (pp. 32-38, first-grade basal reader). Boston: Houghton Mifflin.

Everetts, E., Weiss, B., & Cruickshank, S. (Eds.). (n.d.). Blue bell. In *Can You Imagine?* (Level 6, Holt Basic Reading System,pp. 42-48, first-grade basal reader). New York: Holt, Rinehart & Winston.

Everetts, E., Weiss, B., & Cruickshank, S. (Eds.). (n.d.). Who will play? In *Books and Games* (level 4, Holt Basic Reading System, pp. 43-50, first-grade basal reader). New York: Holt, Rinehart & Winston.

Ferguson, C.A. (1977). Baby talk in six languages. *American Anthropology, 66,* 103-114.

Fredericksen, C.H. (1977). *Inference and the structure of children's discourse.* Paper presented at the symposium on the Development of Discourse Processing Skills, Society for Research in Child Development, New Orleans, LA.

Freebody, P. & Baker, C.D. (1985). Children's first schoolbooks: Introductions to the culture of literacy. *Harvard Educational Review, 55*(4), 381-398.

Gackenbach, D. (1984). *Harry and the terrible whatzit.* New York: Houghton Mifflin.

Gourley, J.W. (1984). Discourse structure: Expectations of beginning readers and readability of text. *Journal of Reading Behavior, 16,*(3), 169-188.

Graff, H.J. (1987). *The legacies of literacy: Continuities and contradictions in Western culture and society.* Bloomington, IN: Indiana University Press.

Halliday, M. (1985). *An introduction to functional grammar.* London: Edward Arnold.

Halliday, M., & Hasan, R. (1976). *Cohesion in English.* London: Longman.

Halliday, M., & Hasan, R. (1980). Text and context: Aspects of language in a social-semiotic perspective. *Sophia Linguistica, 6,* 4-91.

Hansel, P., Borman, K., Redden, L., Moore, R., Bolton, E., Sullivan, M., McDonald, T., Kraft, S., Knipfer, B., Miller, D., Lilly, E., Obermiller, P., Maloney, M., & Mallicoat, A. (in press). Cincinnati's Urban Appalachian Council and Appalachian identity, *Harvard Educational Review.*

Hasan, R. (1979). On the notion of text. In J.S. Petofi (Ed.), *Text vs sentence: Basic questions of text linguistics* (second part). Hamburg: Helmut Buske.

Hasan, R. (1984). Coherence and cohesive harmony. In J. Flood (Ed.), *Understanding reading comprehension* (pp. 181-219). Newark, DE: International Reading Association.

Irwin, J. (1980). The effects of linguistic cohesion on prose comprehension. *Journal of Reading Behavior, 12,* 325-332.

Irwin, J. (1983). Cohesion factors in children's textbooks. *Reading Psychology, 4,* 11-23.

Irwin, J. (1983). Cohesion and comprehension: A research view. In J. Irwin (Ed.), *Understanding and teaching cohesion comprehension* (pp. 31-44). Newark, DE: International Reading Association.

Kintsch, W., & Vipond, D. (1978). Reading comprehension and readability in educational practice and psychological theory. In L.G. Welsson (Ed.), *Memory: Processes and problems.* Hillsdale, NJ: Lawrence Erlbaum.

Lucretius. (65 B.C.?). *De Rerum Natura, IV,* 637.

Marshall, N., & Glock, M. (1978). Comprehension of connected discourse: A study into the relationships between the structure of text and information recalled. *Reading Research Quarterly, 14,* 10-56.

McCoy, C.B., Brown, J.S., & Watkins, V.M. (1981). Implications of changes in Appalachia for urban areas. In W.W. Phillaber & C.B. McCoy (Eds), *The invisible minority: Urban Appalachians.* Lexington: The University Press of Kentucky.

Mikulecky, L.J. (1987). Commentary: Holding it together in the winds of change. *Reading Today, 5*(1), 17.

Moe, A.J., & Irwin, J.W. (1986). Cohesion, coherence and comprehension. In J.W. Irwin (Ed.), *Understanding and teaching cohesion comprehension* (pp. 3-8). Newark, DE: International Reading Association.

Ogbu, J. (1988). Opportunity structures, cultural boundaries and literacy. In J. Langer (Ed.), *Language, literacy and culture: Issues of society and schooling* (pp. 149-177). Norwood, NJ: Ablex.

Pappas, C.C., & Brown, E. (1989). Using turns at story "reading" as scaffolding for learning. *Theory into Practice, XXVIII* (2), 104-113.

Pearson, P.D., & Spiro, K.J. (1980). Toward a theory of reading comprehension instruction. *Topics in Language Disorders, 1,* 71-78.

Rutter, P., & Raban, B. (1982). The development of cohesion in children's writing: A preliminary investigation. *Foreign Language, 3,* 63-75.

Schallert, D.L. (1982). The significance of knowledge: A synthesis of research related to schema theory. In W. Otto & S. White (Eds.), *Reading expository material* (pp. 13-48). New York: Academic Press.

Smith, C.B., & Wardhaugh, R. (1980). *Who can?/Lost and found/Hats and bears* (Series r, Macmillan Reading, Levels 4-6). New York: Macmillan.

Smith, F. (1978). *Reading.* New York: Holt, Rinehart & Winston.

Smitherman, G. (Ed.). (1981). *Black English and the education of black children and youth.* Detroit: Harlo.

Steinberg, C.S., & Bruce, C.B. (1980). Higher level features in children's stories: Rhetorical structure and conflict. In M.L. Kamil & A.J. Moe (Eds.), *Perspective on reading research and instruction* (29th Yearbook of the National Reading Conference). Washington, DC: National Reading Conference.

Taylor, D., & Dorsey-Gaines, C. (1988). *Growing up literate: Learning from inner city families.* Portsmouth, NH: Heinemann.

Ward, M.C. (1971). *Them children, a study in language learning.* New York: Holt.

Wells, G. (1986). *The meaning makers.* Portsmouth, NH: Heinemann.

Wilson, P.T., & Anderson, R.XC. (1985). Reading comprehension and school learning. In J. Osborn, P.T. Wilson, & R.C. Anderson (Eds.), *Reading education: Foundations for a literate America* (pp. 319-328).

Wolfram, W.A., & Christian, D. (1978). Educational implications of dialect diversity. In M.A. Lourie & N.F. Conklin (Eds.), *A pluralistic nation* (pp. 357-381). Rowley, MA: Newbury House.

Wolfram, W.A., & Christian, D. (1976). *Appalachian speech.* Washington: DC: Center for Applied Linguistics.

Zolotow, C. (1962). *Mr. rabbit and the lovely present.* New York: Harper Junior Books.

AUTHOR INDEX

SUBJECT INDEX